BISON
BOOKS

Ojibway Tales

Basil Johnston

University of Nebraska Press
Lincoln and London

First Bison Book printing: 1993
Most recent printing indicated by the last digit below:
10   9   8   7   6   5   4   3

Library of Congress Cataloging-in-Publication Data
Johnston, Basil.
[Moose meat & wild rice]
Ojibway tales / [compiled by] Basil Johnston.
p.   cm.
Originally published: Moose meat & wild rice. Toronto: McClelland and
Stewart, 1978.
ISBN 0-8032-7578-1 (pa)
1. Ojibwa Indians—Fiction.   2. Indians of North America—Canada—
Fiction.   I. Title.
PR9199.3.J597M6   1993
813′.54—dc20
93-2380   CIP

Reprinted by arrangement with Basil Johnston, represented by Allan
Lang, International Book Marketing Limited, New York. Originally pub-
lished in 1978 as *Moose Meat and Wild Rice* by McClelland and Stewart,
Toronto, Ontario.

∞

CONTENTS

Preface

The Moose Meat Point Indian Reserve is populated by about 700 Ojibway. The reserve is like many other Indian reserves; neither prosperous nor severely impoverished; westernized in outward appearance but in soul and spirit very much still Ojibway.

Near by, that is, about twenty or so miles away, is the town of Blunder Bay, a town that once had reason for existence. Its chief claim for recognition today is its unsurpassed understanding of and goodwill toward the natives of Moose Meat Point. Town and reserve are united by a neglected dirt road that is almost unfit for passage by cars.

Moose Meat Point with its 30,000 acres, is isolated, unprepossessing, somewhat less than paradise, but it is home. Since its founding in the 1840s, Moose Meaters have gone from the reserve for various purposes and for varying lengths of time. They have always returned, as they will always return, no matter what. Moose Meat Point is home.

By the time Moose Meaters were herded onto the reserve they had already adopted a number of West European customs, techniques, and approaches into their way of life. Some were imposed upon them. Once incarcerated on the reserve, Moose Meat Indians were expected to advance even more quickly. Missionaries came and government agents were assigned to assist in, hasten, and ensure the success of their advance.

As eager as they were to acquire what the white man had to offer, Moose Meaters had difficulty understanding and deciding upon the relative merits of "Brand X" religion and "Brand X" politics. They espoused as many religions as were available to them, only to find that the different faiths were as divisive for Moose Meaters as they were for the white man. Politics produced the same results. Moose Meaters tried to abide by the laws, moral and civil, general and special that were enacted and administered for their own good while trying to keep some of their customs and values alive. However, Moose Meaters could observe one and find themselves breaking another.

As time went by, game diminished and Moose Meaters were forced to go outside the reserve more frequently to seek employment. In their excursions into the white man's world, Moose Meaters discovered more about the white man and his new and startling inventions, which they eagerly imported to the reserve upon their inevitable return.

But many, like the oyster in "The Walrus and The Carpenter" who chose not to leave his oyster bed, were content to remain in Moose Meat Point where they could live without interference, and in their own fashion, deal with the white man and his peculiar ways; accept, reject, or modify whatever was brought into the village.

More years passed during which the Ojibway in the isolation of Moose Meat Point made little headway. Moose Meaters remained on the reserve and they remained unpolished and unlettered. A school was built and a teacher was hired. With fine manners, acumen, and a good command of English, young Moose Meaters and Moose Meat Point could expect better things.

But things did not get better either on or off the reserve. Better English, service in war, correct deportment, the right to vote, proper dress, social graces, and even new insights did not enhance conditions or the circumstances of the people of Moose Meat Point, nor improve their relations with white people.

Instead, matters seemed to get worse. Unemployment was high, housing poor, general health was bad, and education was eschewed.

Something had to be done. In recent years, the Indian Affairs Branch devised all sorts of programs and handed out grants, left, right and centre to remedy the ills. The provincial government, too, tried to horn in by offering formulae and prescriptions for progress and success. Universities and museums began research in earnest and offered courses. Citizens began clamoring for abolition, education, integration, solution, assimilation, co-operation, and, of course, damnation.

While many aspects of Indian life changed over the years,

8

the basic nature of the Ojibway of Moose Meat Point remained essentially the same. They were individualistic, resourceful, informal, proud, impulsive, imaginative, practical, independent, perceptive, patient, and above all, possessed a wonderful sense of humour. As long as they retained their language, they retained their sense of fun and wit. Unhappily, the language is vanishing.

During the same time, the white man also has remained unchanged. Though he may intend good, the white man has too often allowed his sense of order, organization, superiority, his fondness for paperwork, efficiency, convention, ceremony, change, his penchant for formula, prescription, solution, and his haste, overbearing, force, and decisiveness to negate his intentions.

Such then is the background and the setting for the events that make up the story of the Ojibway of Moose Meat Point in their relationships with the West Europeans and in their attempts to adopt some aspects of West European culture and to keep alive some of their own.

In one sense this story is a kind of a history although it is not intended to be such. Rather, it is intended primarily as an amusing account of Indian-white man relationships.

We are indebted to Tom McCue, Albert Belleau, Harold Belleau, Fred Green, Xavier Michon, Rufus Johnston (my father), Norman Jones, Victor Johnson (deceased), Mike Trudeau (deceased), Eugene Keeshig, Jean Shawana, Joe Peter Pangwish, Gregor Keeshig, Lillian Nadjiwon, dear friends and fellow Moose-Meaters, and to the Ojibway for these accounts.

I dedicate this book to story-tellers, listeners and to all good Moose Meat people; to those with a sense of humour; to Anna Porter and my editor who can smile and giggle; I dedicate this book especially to the white man, without whose customs and evangelistic spirit the events recounted would not have occurred.

PART 1

THE RESOURCEFULNESS OF THE MOOSE MEAT POINT OJIBWAY

Indian Smart: Moose Smart

Six Moose Meat Point Indians, in two canoes, were returning home unhappy from an abortive hunting expedition at the far end of Porcupine Yellow Liver Lake. They were weary from several days of trekking through bush devoid of game, and hungry from a half a day of paddling on empty stomachs. The coming winter would be thin.

"Hey! What's that in the water ahead?" asked Madawayash (Whistling Wind) lifting himself up straighter on his knees and pointing to a tiny object in the water a mile or so ahead of them.

Everybody stopped paddling. All six, four men and two women, squinted into the autumn sunlight made brighter by the rippling and dancing of the sun-drenched lake. They shaded their eyes to reduce the glare. What the object was they could not tell for certain, but they began to speculate.

"Maybe it's a sea serpent," quavered Sweet Plum, Whistling Wind's wife.

"Nah. Don't think so. Ain't none around these parts," Whistling Wind assured her, continuing to look.

"It's something big anyhow, and it's swimming," observed Thick Blanket sitting down on his haunches. "Can't really tell until we get some closer."

"Come on. Paddle," Whistling Wind invited and encouraged his companions. He dipped his paddle into the water and strained. The others likewise paddled furiously.

After a long period of fierce paddling, the Moose Meaters, brows dripping with sweat, halted for a breather. They all strained forward to attain a sharper glimpse of the object ahead.

Aessaence (Little Shell), the oldest and keenest of eye in the group drew in his breath.

"There's two of'em!" he gasped in astonishment. "Either deer or moose. Can't tell. Too far away yet."

"Come on! Let's go! Paddle! What are we waiting for?" Whistling Wind commanded, plunging his paddle into the water, and sending the lead canoe pitching forward. The Moose Meaters dug in their paddles, whisking the water backward in little sprays. No one spoke as the canoes knifed keenly through the waters. There was only the sound of heavy breathing, and dip, swish, dip, swish.

"Have a little rest," Whistling Wind suggested setting his paddle across the gunwales and wiping his brow with his shirt-tail. The others stopped paddling, breathing hard.

"It's two moose!" Whistling Wind cried out triumphantly. "Meat tonight! Come on! Don't stop!"

The Moose Meaters resumed paddling at once. Nor did they pause until they drew up immediately behind the two great animals, male and female, which were swimming power-fully toward a point barely discernible in the distance.

The female moose turned her head partway around and rolled an eye at them. She strained forward, the male following without glancing back.

The Indians relaxed a bit, paddling less frantically.

"I get the heart," Whistling Wind said, claiming the choi-cest morsel of moose innards.

"I want the liver," shrilled Sweet Plum, whose ample pro-portions showed a connoisseur's appetite.

And everyone claimed a part; the kidneys, a steak, a roast, a rump roast. No one would go unsatisfied. Mouths moistened, and stomachs rumbled.

"I'm tired. Why can't we get that moose to pull us?" asked Sleeping Water in the second canoe.

"Be damned. Never thought of that, me," Whistling Wind replied with excitement.

"Hey! Check and see. We got a rope in front?"

Thick Blanket, sitting in the first canoe, rummaged around and found a rope some twenty-five feet in length. He showed it to Whistling Wind.

"Make a lasso. We'll throw it around the moose's neck," Whistling Wind suggested.

"Don't! You better not," Sweet Plum protested. "It's bad enough we gonna kill that moose; don't have to make fun of him."

"That's right" Aessaence agreed. "Bring us bad luck. Just leave him."

"We're not gonna make fun of him," Whistling Wind corrected. "We're just gonna make him work. He's gonna die anyhow. Might as well work."

But Sweet Plum was not able to see the irrefutable logic of this. "I don't think it's right, me," she said shaking her head morosely.

"Lasso's ready," shouted Thick Blanket.

"Okay! We'll move alongside the moose. You slip the lasso over the moose's antlers and then we'll drop back," Whistling Wind instructed.

Turning around Whistling Wind outlined his plan to those in the second canoe. "And when we get that rope on the moose you guys gonna get a ride too, so you'd better throw us up another rope before we start. After that the moose'll go so fast you guys'll never catch up," he finished.

Consequently the canoes were fastened together.

"Okay, get ready," Whistling Wind yelled to Thick Blanket, who spread the rope with his fingers.

Whistling Wind paddled hard. The canoe drew up to the moose. All Thick Blanket had to do was to slip the noose around the moose's great antlers. It was all so simple.

As the rope tightened around his antlers, and the moose felt the whole weight of the two canoes and their passengers, the great beast shook his head from side to side to throw it off. Now the rope was firmly caught and his best efforts could not dislodge it. The moose snorted and rolled his eyes, began to gather speed.

The canoes fell back the length of the rope. The Moose Meaters sat back and relaxed.

"Better watch out. Water's pretty shallow 'round here," Emmanual Buckshot cautioned. "Many shoals."

"No shoals around here," Whistling Wind retorted with a laugh. "Been fishin' an' huntin' in these parts for years and I ain't found none yet."

"Better be careful," said Aessaence looking over the side of the canoe.

"Have a good rest," Whistling Wind advised his companions. "Got a long way to go yet. Then we gotta set up camp and butcher this moose. Hard work." He filled and lit his pipe before sitting back to enjoy the leisure.

"Yeah, just like white man," Whistling Wind mused as he

sucked on his pipe. "Wonder how come Indians never got moose or deer to pull things. Boy, if they could see us now they wouldn't think Indians were so stupid," he chortled.

"Yeah," Thick Blanket agreed. "White man thinks he's so smart because horses is stupid."

"Indian smart; moose smart," Whistling Wind observed self-righteously, spitting in the lake.

Banter continued back and forth between the crews as they approached the point.

Whistling Wind took out his rifle, raised it to his shoulder.

"Get your head down, Thick Blanket," he commanded.

"What for?" asked Thick Blanket turning around, and looking into the barrel of the rifle. He dropped down in fright.

"Just wanna take a bead," Whistling Wind explained, squinting hard. "Pow, right through the head." He grinned and put down the rifle.

"Better get a knife ready to cut the rope pretty soon now. You duck when I tell you, okay?"

Thick Blanket gulped, and nodded.

"Gettin' pretty shallow. I can see bottom," Emmanual warned.

Everyone looked over the side fascinated.

"Hey, I can see some fish," Thick Blanket said ecstatically. "Where? Where?" came the chorus. They peered down more closely.

Distracted as they were, the hollow choomp caught them unaware. The canoe lurched forward in short, rapid jerks. The Moose Meaters looked up in astonishment.

The moose, water dripping from his antlers and flanks, had found footing, and was making his way swiftly to land.

"Eeeeeeyauh"' screamed Sweet Plum.

The moose tossed his antlers to shake off the rope, and kicked his hind feet in the air, sending up sprays of water and mud into the face of Thick Blanket who yelled out in shock.

"Cut the rope! Cut the rope!" Whistling Wind shouted.

"I can't! I can't see anything!" Thick Blanket bawled, trying to wipe the muddy water out of his eyes.

"Shoot him! Shoot him!" Aessaence bellowed.

But the moose was now galloping as best and as fast as he could while pulling two canoes loaded with six Moose Meat Point Indians.

"Shoot 'im! Shoot 'im!" Emmanual Buckshot pleaded.

"I'm trying! I'm trying!" muttered Whistling Wind as he

16

tried to draw a steady bead.

Thick Blanket's head jerked into the line of fire.

"Get your head outa the way!" he commanded. "Sit down, woman!" Whistling Wind ordered Sweet Plum, who was trying to scramble out of the canoe in her panic.

Both dropped down at once, Thick Blanket gripping the gunwales desperately, Sweet Plum emitting little moans of terror.

The moose continued straight ahead.

Whistling Wind straightened his back, and drew an unsteady, wet bead on the beast; and the moose, as if sensing his execution was at hand, darted to the left. The bullet whined past his ear. He jerked.

The canoe keeled over dumping Thick Blanket and Sweet Plum unceremoniously into the water.

At the sound of the shot, the moose had snorted in fright, kicked out his hind legs once, twice, three times, before increasing his speed.

Whistling Wind had been deposited in the water along with Sweet Plum and Thick Blanket. He had done his best to keep the rifle dry, but had only succeeded in breaking the stock on the stony bottom of the lake. Now he could only sit and swear helplessly at the running moose.

The occupants of the second canoe abandoned ship helter-skelter, yielding possession of the craft to the moose.

His burden lighter, the moose trumpeted triumphantly, bounded up the rocky shore following his mate, who was slightly in the lead, the canoes bouncing and scraping, cracking and crackling behind them.

Dragging two canoes that would not come loose, the great bull charged into the thicket in a cloud of pebbles, branches, broken sticks, an assortment of pots, pans, and supplies, and splinters of canoe ribs and bark. For sure the animals would not be hard to track.

The six Moose Meat Point Indians gathered up various personal chattels in the cold October waters, picked up little bundles that floated to the surface, retrieved sodden tams, and made their way dripping to the shore, looking and feeling dejected and forlorn.

"Guess you know now why Indians never got moose to pull things, eh?" Aessaence remarked with cold irony to the shivering Whistling Wind.

"Yeah! If white man could only see us now," said Emmanual Buckshot sarcastically.

"Oh, shut up!" was all Whistling Wind could manage through his chattering teeth.

"If You Want to Play"

"If you want to play, look for an Ojibway," best sums up the good opinion that other people had formed of the members of that tribe. The Ojibway were friendly, handsome, vigorous, and resourceful by reputation, especially the Moose Meat species. On the band lists of many other reserves in Canada and the United States are the names of numerous fair maidens from Moose Meat Point; proof of the demand for the companionship of Moose Meat women. And that Moose Meat men have imported as their wives women of numerous nationalities– English, Delaware, German, Cree, Mohawk, and Dutch–is a tribute to the general merit of the romantic abilities and powers of persuasion of these dauntless Ojibway. They came. They saw. And they did not stop until they had conquered.

Wherever they went, whatever they did, the Ojibway were welcome. Their arrival was eagerly awaited, their stay long remembered. Every one of them did something to uphold and sustain the good opinion and add to the reputation they had gained.

Luffus was no exception–in fact he may have excelled his compatriots in many respects. He was gregarious, always helpful, industrious, outgoing, and an exceptionally hard worker who spent most of his winters in lumber camps far to the west.

One winter, Luffus went as far west as White River, to work cutting jack pine and tamarack for the Abitibi Power and Paper Company in one of their lumber camps. A few other Indians were there; a couple of Crees and some Ojibway.

In no time, Luffus became the friend of one of them, Jack Fish-Eyes, a northern Ojibway who had established a winter camp with other local Ojibway families some ten miles from the lumbering operation. Jack Fish-Eyes and his friends went home week-ends; Luffus was compelled to remain in the camp, since his home was too far away.

However, it was not long before Jack Fish-Eyes invited Luffus to Sunday dinner. "Come eat with us," he said, "but don't expect anything fancy. We ain't got much, but we'd like to have you visit us anyhow."

"O.K." said Luffus, accepting the invitation readily.

Very early one Sunday morning the party set out for the encampment, the snow squeaking under their feet and their breaths puffing up little white clouds. The men, weary from the late night before, eyes watering from the cold, arrived at the campsite around ten in the morning to the welcoming barks of dogs and the giggles of small children. Five tents were pitched in a semi-circle around a central campfire which crackled briskly. Over the fire was a horizontal pole, some eight or ten feet in length supported at either end by two other poles, crossed and bound six feet above the ground. From the horizontal pole were suspended chains and wires bearing black cast iron cooking pots of various sizes. The other four men greeted by their families went to their respective lodgings. Luffus went with Jack Fish-Eyes.

In the tent which was comfortably warm, spotlessly clean and neat, Luffus was introduced to Pearl, Jack's wife. She went to the fire to put on water for tea at once. Luffus, as guest, was a trifle alarmed at the noticeable lack of food of any kind inside the lodge; neither had he observed any animal carcasses outside, although he had looked covertly while walking into camp. Soon warmed by the tea, he began to talk and he regaled his hosts with stories and accounts of reserve life on Moose Meat Point. How his hosts marvelled. They even expressed some envy for the lucky Indians who lived on the Moose Meat Point Reserve. Many cups of tea were passed around.

It was in the afternoon, far beyond the normal mealtime when Jack asked his wife to prepare a meal.

"Let's eat."

Pearl went into action. She called to the others, her voice booming out over the camp. Presently, the men, the women, and the children crowded into Jack's tent. Luffus was introduced to the entire community. During the introductions, Pearl, assisted by the other women removed two potato sacks from the corner and took them outside.

20

"Come on. Come and watch." Jack invited Luffus outside. Jack, Luffus, and the other men went out and stood in the cold watching the women.

Pearl erected several sapling sticks at irregular intervals on the snow. When she was finished, the other women extracted a net from one of the sacks, unrolled it, then spread it out, lacing the mesh over the stakes until the entire net was evenly suspended about three feet above the surface of the snow. Pearl tied one end of the border of the net and extended the other end along the surface and into her tent through a slit. Finally, the women brought out a small sack, from which they broadcast wheat on the snow beneath the net.

"O.K. Let's go in." Pearl commanded entering the tent. Everybody went in and sat down.

A child began to whisper.

"Shshshshshsh!" Pearl insisted.

No one spoke again.

Luffus was puzzled. He watched Pearl, who knelt in the corner of the tent, looking out the slit.

Presently he heard the flutter of wings, and the twitters and cheeps of hundreds of birds. Pearl did not move. The fluttering diminished; the twitters and cheeps increased.

"Ahow," (O.K.) Pearl grunted, pulling the rope that she grasped in her hand, as she rose from her cramped position. Immediately the fluttering and twittering increased in pitch and intensity.

Pearl led the other women outside; the men and the children followed.

Luffus was astounded by what he observed. Dozens of birds, snow-birds, chickadees, juncos, were cheeping and chirping frantically, flapping their wings desperately in an attempt to escape their entanglement in the mesh. The women immediately began to disentangle the birds from the net. With a flick of the wrist the women detached the heads from the bodies, the latter of which they placed in a pile. The youngsters plucked the birds, then threw them into another pile.

While the women and children were busy with the birds, the men stoked the fire with kindling and dried cedar logs until it was roaring. By the time the logs had burned down to a bed of glowing coals, the women and children had finished their task, and had placed the birds close to the fire. Luffus was given a long stick. Following the example of the others he skewered a snow-bird, and barbecued it slowly, turning it over several times. Never having eaten any bird smaller than a partridge, he was dubious about the experiment. Nevertheless, his hunger overcame his doubts.

Luffus ate. The birds were delicious. Seldom had he eaten anything so fine. He ate many more chickadees, juncos and snow-birds.

After the winter picnic, when everyone was filled according to his capacity, all went into the lodge.

Luffus, feeling grateful and expansive after the delicious meal, offered to teach Pearl the formula for making wine, a recipe developed by the Moose Meat Indians, whose talent and resourcefulness in this art have never been fully recognized nor appreciated.

Pearl brightened at the thought of expanding her culinary knowledge.

"You need a couple of pounds of beans. Soak them in water overnight," Luffus disclosed. "You boil them after that for a couple of hours. Strain off the juice. Put some raisins in the juice, coupla yeast cakes after it gets pretty cool, and a coupla cups a sugar. Put the stuff in jars, and cover them jars with blankets. You got to keep the stuff warm for mebbe three days 'fore it's any good to drink," he instructed as he sipped on his tea.

Pearl memorized the instructions, admiring Luffus for his learning.

Although she was eager to try her new recipe, Pearl bemoaned her lack of even the most basic ingredients, especially the sealers.

Luffus promised to bring everything with him on the following week, since he had been asked to visit again.

As she went about her business, Pearl expressed her sentiments about Luffus. "He's such a nice man, knows so many stories, so many things, not like some of the bums Jack brings home." The other ladies agreed.

All that week Luffus cultivated the acquaintance and the confidence of the camp cook. At the end of the week he was able to persuade the cook to provide the beans, yeast cake and sugar, and the raisins, saying that he was going to make Boston Baked Beans Indian style with raisins. As an afterthought he asked for some lemons. The cook raised his eyebrows, scratched his head and marvelled at the intestinal fortitude of Indian people. And why would anyone want to make Boston Baked Beans in the two dozen sealers which Luffus had also requested? No matter;

the cook was a tolerant man, willing to overlook cultural differences.

Sunday, Luffus and Jack took the ingredients to the encampment. Again they feasted on the delicate flesh of the small birds. Just before returning to the lumber camp, Luffus repeated his instructions to Pearl, suggesting that she begin to soak the beans on Wednesday, boiling the essential nectar from the beans on Thursday, after which she would mix in the other ingredients into the strained juice. Luffus warned her repeatedly to cool the mixture before adding the yeast, but once the yeast had been added, warmth was necessary for fermentation. By Sunday, Luffus hoped, the brew would have obtained its most exhilarating, potent excellence, and Luffus would sample the fruits of Pearl's skill as a brewmaster.

That evening Luffus and the other men trudged back to the Abitibi bunk houses to work and wait for the week to pass.

On Wednesday, as instructed, Pearl began operations, watched and assisted by the other ladies. She followed her instructions to the letter.

By Thursday evening Pearl's tent was befumed with the sweet penetrating odour of fermenting bean wine. She crinkled her nose as she poured the stuff into the sealers, sniffed loudly, and coughed. She had never smelled anything quite like this. Would the pungency keep her awake she wondered?

Just before retiring Pearl filled the last jar and closed it tightly. She checked all of the jars swaddled in blankets. It had been a long day and Pearl slept well.

The next morning her first act was to check the bottles again. All was well. Many of the sealers showed signs of bubbling as Luffus had said they would. Because the odour seemed to have cleared off during the night, Pearl went about her tasks happily, secure in the knowledge that she had followed the recipe exactly. Pearl did not check the bottles again.

Pearl's days were long and tiring. Everyone else had retired that night, when Pearl turned down the lantern, and snuggled into the blankets. She drifted off to sleep.

BOOM! A muffled explosion. Pearl's eyes flew open. That sounded like a gun!

BOOM! BOOM! It was close by! Pearl sat bolt upright, wide awake.

BOOM! The sound was coming from within the tent!

BOOM! Pearl screamed.

BOOM! BOOM! BOOM! The dreaded Bearwalker!

Pearl ran out of the tent shrieking. The women ran out of the other tents, and chattered at her excitedly.

"What's the matter?"

"What happened?"

"Why are you making all that noise?"

This they demanded of poor Pearl who shivered from the cold and her fright. All she could do was point her shaking finger in the direction of the tent, and heave, unable to speak.

BOOM! BOOM! Faint outside but audible.

The ladies shuddered.

Another muffled report resounded through the icy air.

The ladies shivered once more. Pearl began to cry.

One old crone who had given up fear many years ago hobbled to the tent.

BOOM! BOOM! The blasts seemed to have gained violence.

One distraught lady wailed, "Stop her! She'll be killed."

The old lady poked her head out of the flap of the tent.

"It's O.K." she said. "It's only that wine. It's all busting out."

BOOM! BOOM! emphasized the exploding bottles.

"It's that Luffus. He tried to kill us. If we'da drunk that stuff we'da all've busted wide open, just like them jars. Huh! My it stinks in here!" she said wheezing as she emerged.

The women entered the tent, now reeking from the sweetish fumes of the fermented liquid. With the help of her neighbours Pearl cleaned the blankets of sticky raisins and splintered glass, and hung them outside to air and dry.

Pearl clenched her teeth and stuck out her jaw. "I don't want that man here any more. I hope that husband of mine doesn't bring him home again on Sunday. If he does I'm not cooking for him."

The other ladies nodded their heads in agreement. Pearl was right.

Early Sunday morning Jack got up to visit his family.

"Come on Luffus, let's go," Jack invited cheerfully, shaking the snoring Luffus.

Luffus moaned as he opened his eyes. He could only speak in a hoarse whisper. His throat hurt when he spoke.

"I'm sick. Go on without me," he croaked, coughing.

"That's too bad. Well, next Sunday then. I'll bring you some wine," promised Jack.

Luffus nodded, and pulled the blankets up to his chin. His head pounded. He shivered. All during the day he slept, but at nightfall, feeling somewhat restored he got up and dressed.

Jack returned to camp later that evening. He seemed uncommonly subdued and unfriendly to Luffus, who was anxious to hear about the wine.

"Where's my wine?" he asked.

"Don't you speak to me any more."

Turning to the other men in the camp Jack said, "This man here tried to kill us. Made some of his wine and all the sealers bust up."

Luffus smote his forehead, groaning. He knew what had happened. He tried to explain.

"You don't close those lids tight."

Silence.

He tried to apologize, to make amends.

"Sorry, Jack. I thought I told you not to close them up."

Silence.

Eventually he regained Jack's friendship, but no further invitations for a feast of snow-birds were ever issued.

The Honey Pot

"Hey, dere's a bee's nes' back dere. Bedder watch out for it when you go back," Tikip (Cool Water, or Spring) advised his companions casually.

"Where?" asked Shigun (Bass) with sudden interest as he pulled from the fire a pan of salt pork, eggs and scone he had been frying. He wiped both sides of his hands along his pants in an unconscious signal that the meal was ready.

"Back dere about a hunnerd yards," replied Tikip, sitting down on his side of the frying pan and picking up his fork.

Adam and Shigun took their places, satisfying their hunger from opposite sides of the common frying pan. For several minutes the three ate in companionable silence, broken only by the crackling of the fire and the buzz of flies.

"What kinda bees, anyhow?" Shigun wanted to know.

"Honey bees," muttered Tikip, pouring himself a burst of tea from a tin pail blackened by the smoke of many fires. "Living in an ol' cedar stump dem."

Shigun's interest was thoroughly aroused.

"Haven't had good honey for twen' mebbee tirty years," he mused through a mouthful of crisp scone. "Only had dat bought stuff."

Shigun continued to reflect as the men finished their breakfast.

"Come on, Tikip" he said when he had rolled a cigarette to his satisfaction. "Show us where dat honey is at."

Tikip meandered from the shore into the bush followed by Adam and Shigun. Ten yards from a stump, Tikip hesitated. He circled the stump silently, halted, and pointed.

"Dere," he said with the pride of great discovery.

The three men regarded the stump in curiosity. And, as if to confirm Tikip's declaration of their existence and presence, a few bees emerged from between the roots to buzz menacingly near them. The men backed away hastily.

"Hmm," said Shigun. "Yeah. Mebbee we can take dat honey. Make a good meal dat, and we could split what's left tree ways."

They walked thoughtfully back to the shore. All the while Shigun cleaned his pans, he tempted his comrades with thoughts about the goodness of honey. Not only did honey sweeten tea to ambrosia, it turned scone into cake of the finest delicacy. A little honey was good for the flagging energies of man, woman, and child. It turned a meal into a veritable feast.

Adam and Tikip listened, were intrigued, were convinced.

"Hell," said Tikip looking at the swale, "We'll never be able to get t'rough dat stuff."

"Yeah," declared Adam wistfully. "Can't smoke 'em out, neider. Too close to de ground."

"Granddad always said when bees live close to the ground like dat, gonna be easy winter," reflected Tikip.

Shigun, aware that he had convinced his companions, stayed quiet during the interchange. Now he moved in to scatter any remaining objections.

"Been tinkin'," he mused. "Bet I know how to get dat honey."

"How?" asked Tikip, astonished.

"Easy. Since we can't smoke 'em out, bes' way is de direc' attack. We got oilers (fisherman's rubber coat and pants). Dey'll do fer coverin' up. Alls we need is a head net and some mitts. An' if you," turning to Tikip, "put 'em on you get enough protection so's you won' get stung. You go in dere wid an axe, chop open dat stump real fast an' . . . "

"Old cedar stump gonna be as hard as a bullet," Tikip moaned.

"Strong guy like you, split it open real easy, I bet," said Shigun with inescapable logic. "Anyhow, den you scoop out dat honey in dis bucket and run back out fas'. Dem bees ain't gonna hurt you. Me and Adam, we'll wait for you about half-way 'n swat dem bees wit' bags or sumpin'. Beat 'em off."

"Now just a damn minute there," Tikip broke in. "I ain't going. What am I gonna use for a head net 'n mitts?"

"Got a couple of potato sacks here we'll use. Just the ting. Wrap 'em around your head and make two holes fer eyes. Bees won't get t'rough dem." So saying, Shigun went to the boat and extracted four old potato bags redolent of long dead fish.

"Hell, Adam can go! He runs faster den me!"

"Can't neider," Adam disclaimed. "Why don't you go?" he asked old Shigun.

"Me? Too old. Too slow. Legs bodder me lots in the damp wedder. Look, if you want dat honey we gotta get it today, 'fore somebody else comes along 'n steals it. Let's make a big fire smudge right here, den when you comes out you can stand in de smoke. Bees never bodder you den. Smoke puts 'em right to sleep. Besides, dey ain't gonna get dis far. Dey can only fly about half-way here. My grandfader–or somebody–used to say dat if you run fast you can outrun bees anytime. Do it myself, except I can't run anymore."

"He's right, Adam," Tikip put in. "Teacher tol' me once dat, bees weren't made for flying at all. Too heavy in de ass. Wonder dey can get off de ground," he said.

"Come on, Adam," wheedled Shigun. "You do it. You can have half de honey. Me and Tikip'll share the rest."

Adam wavered. "But it's tick in there. Can't run out very fast."

"We'll make a trail den," said Shigun cheerfully, confidently, and decisively.

Adam reluctantly agreed.

The men grabbed their axes and hacked away at limbs and saplings until a pathway was cleared from the bee's nest to the rocky shore.

Adam put on the oilers, and stood as still as an artist's model while Tikip and Shigun draped the old potato sacks around his head, securing them with clothesline rope.

"Cheeze, ever look like a scarecrow, you," Tikip giggled, and wrinkling his nose at the odour of ancient cargoes of fish emitted by the potato bags, added, "Don't smell so good neider."

"You want dat honey, you better shut up," Adam said testily.

"Hey! Where's dem mitts?"

"Oh yeah! Nearly forgot about dat." And Shigun produced yet another bag, which he cut into strips with his jack-knife.

Hand coverings were quickly fashioned.

Adam was ready. Like some great faceless beast he stood, in one hand an axe, in the other a bucket. He shook his head for better vision in the improvised, evil-smelling mask.

"Damn bees don't get me, de smell will," he grumbled, sweating.

All three entered the bush. Shigun and Tikip stopped halfway down the newly made trail and armed themselves with willow branches. They took their positions on either side of the pathway, waiting.

Adam stomped off, an erstwhile Frankenstein monster from the woods bent on frightening the bees to death it appeared.

Shigun looked after his creation with pride.

The crash, wham, and chop of the axe resounded through the woods. Complete silence followed. The men braced themselves.

"Eeeeeeyawh, eeeyawh, eeeeeeyawh!" came Adam's muffled screams. The crunch of steps, snap of twigs, and the swish of whipping branches preceded Adam, who burst out of the inner bush, pursued by a swarm of irate bees, buzzing ominously. Gone was the axe and pail. His mask had slipped perilously far over his eyes blinding him, and he tore at it as he passed by Shigun and Tikip.

"Eeeeeeyawh!" he screamed again, as another defender of the hive found a tender spot on the victim.

Shigun and Tikip looked at one another in astonishment. What could have gone wrong? True to their word they chased after Adam's retreating back, now covered with a writhing mass of furious bees, raining a shower of blows upon him. The bees, as if by pre-arranged plan, split, and formed two additional squadrons, the better to attack Shigun and Tikip as well.

"Eeeeyawh!" gasped Adam.

"Eeeeyawh!" Tikip screamed.

"EEEeeeyawh!" bellowed Shigun.

Out of the bush, arms flailing, legs churning, ran the honey thieves. They passed by the fire and its smoke, heading straight into the water, sending up spray after spray in their frantic haste. The bees attacked again and again, not tired by distance, nor discouraged by the willow branches. The men dove into the water, came up, were attacked again. Back under they went. They surfaced yelling, cursing, and hitting out at the bees. The din was fearsome.

At this precise moment of total surrender, with the bees carrying the day, a boatload of tourists trolling for trout came around a point of land. One sharp-eyed lady with binoculars not involved in fishing beheld the drama taking place near the shore. She gasped in astonishment and horror.

"Oh! Murder! Murder!" she howled. "They're *killing* each other!"

"Where? Where?" asked many voices from the crowd with avid bloodlust.

"There! Over there! By the shore!" she sputtered, pointing shoreward. All eyes turned.

"Oh My God! She's right! Those Indians are killing one another," a man exclaimed.

"No, its two men doing the killing! Two against one!" wailed the lady with the binoculars. "Blood-thirsty savages!"

She shook her fist, dislodging her broad brimmed hat which floated away unnoticed.

"They've got him in the water and he's DOWN. There he comes, up again. They're hitting him, and he's Down!" Like a sportscaster at a boxing match she kept up a running commentary for her fellow passengers, who could not see as well as she because of the distance. Leaning over the side to observe the carnage more closely, she waited for the first blood to be drawn. She licked her lips in anticipation.

The operator of the boat revved up the kicker as he turned the boat around. Fishing could never compete with such real-life action.

"We'd better phone the police," he said in excitement.

Next day, two constables arrived on the reserve making discreet inquiries. They went to the Indian Agent's residence first.

"Any Indians missing around here?" asked the Corporal astutely.

"No," the agent replied in astonishment. "Are there supposed to be?"

"Well, we got it on good authority that a man was murdered by two other men yesterday. Actually saw the murder taking place on the shore. One guy was in the water DOWN."

The agent was startled into action; accompanying the two officers he made diligent inquiries at each house on the reserve to determine whether or not anyone was gone.

But no one was missing. It was true that three men were in the Blunder Bay Hospital undergoing treatment for severe bee stings but they were expected to survive the ordeal.

The officers continued to conduct their investigation over the next few days. When they failed to turn up either evidence or body, they submitted a written report on the alleged murder.

"Unsolved," it stated definitely. "Indians unco-operative. All those interviewed pleaded ignorance."

Shigun, Tikip and Adam refused honey for their toast all during their stay in the hospital.

The Potatoes Musta Fell Out

Kokopiness (Owl Bird) was a prosperous farmer on the Moose Meat Point Indian Reserve. Better off than most, he kept his larder, cellar and pits filled with carrots, pumpkins, turnips and potatoes. Preserves were always at hand. His family did not want.

When autumn came Kokopiness, his wife, Margaret, and his family filled sealers with fruits and bins with vegetables. Potatoes and apples were stored in pits at the back of his farm.

The produce from the harvest had always been sufficient to sustain Kokopiness and his family throughout the long winter months and enable him to sell a little of the surplus.

The earth was good and the seasons were certain. Plant in the spring; hope for enough rain in summer; wait and watch the plants grow; harvest in the autumn the product of rain, fertility, labour and sweat. The earth would yield. In winter eat the abundance.

When one was as industrious as Kokopiness, one did not have to worry about food. When the land was as bountiful as his and the seasons were reliable, there was a certain degree of confidence.

Kokopiness was sitting in a rocking chair watching the March snow melt. He was getting hungry for the meal his wife was about to prepare.

"We need some more potatoes. We don't have any in the house," she communicated in Ojibway.

Kokopiness got up. In the shed he lifted a pick-axe and a spade. He proceeded to the back of the farm where his potato pits were located.

But when he got to the pits Kokopiness stopped in shock. A mound of earth encircled each of the pits in a broken and peaked ring. Neither pit contained a solitary potato.

Kokopiness was puzzled. He could not figure it out. How had his potatoes disappeared? Perhaps someone had purloined them. But still he was puzzled. Why would anyone want to steal his potatoes? They had never done so before. People had always asked for potatoes, and, when he had a small surplus he had given them freely. In puzzlement Kokopiness shook his head.

He went back to the house deep in thought.

"Where are the potatoes?" rasped his wife.

"Gone," replied Kokopiness shrugging his shoulders.

"Gone where? Whatta you mean?" asked Kokopiness' wife, adjusting her faded wine tam in puzzlement.

"Gone! Gone!" repeated Kokopiness in a louder voice. He extended his hands outward, palms up.

"You mean stole?" questioned the woman as she pulled up a stocking that had been failed by her garter.

"Maybe." Kokopiness acknowledged the possibility.

"Someone took them?" The woman made an ineffective grab for the other stocking that also threatened imminent collapse.

"Yeah! Maybe someone took them, I guess. Both pits didn't have no potatoes. All gone. Dirt all heaped up. Boards gone too." Kokopiness scratched his head.

"Whatcha gonna do?"

"Dunno." Kokopiness was still trying to figure out what had happened to the potatoes.

"You better do something. There ain't nothing to eat," insisted his wife.

Kokopiness could only nod his head. The pace of the day's events was too fast for him.

"Mebee you should go over to Pitwaniquot's (Between the Clouds) place and borrow some potatoes," she hinted. To her, the most startling realization of all was that there was not enough to eat. Many years of life with Kokopiness had taught her that he would eventually find some explanation for the disappearance of the potatoes, but until then he would not look for a solution to the problem. How long it would take she did not know. In the meantime she did not plan to go hungry.

"Ain't gonna borrow no potatoes. People gonna laugh at me," returned Kokopiness. He took a pinch of snuff and stuffed it between his lower lip and his teeth.

"You have to do something," added Mrs. Kokopiness. "We ain't got no potatoes, us. We gotta eat; the kids gotta eat."

"I know," said Kokopiness knowledgeably.

"Then you gonna have to get some relief," offered Mrs. Kokopiness, hitching up her sagging corset in determination.

Kokopiness recognized the gesture. He knew his wife was resolute.

"Can't do that. People'd laugh at me," argued Kokopiness, lifting the lid of the stove and spitting a streak of tobacco juice into its glowing interior.

Mrs. Kokopiness shifted her wine tam ominously. "Then I'm gonna go to the Council meeting on Monday and ask for relief."

Kokopiness almost choked on the rest of his snuff. He could not allow his wife to go to the Council meeting to ask for relief. Who knows what she would say or what she would do?

"What you want me to do? What you want me to say?" With resignation Kokopiness asked for guidance.

"Well, you ask for relief, mebee a hunnert dollars. Enough to buy food till spring," Mrs. Kokopiness counselled.

Kokopiness nodded.

On Monday Kokopiness went to the Council meeting in the village. Many people crowded into the Council Hall; the chief, the Councillors, the agent, assorted petitioners, and several white men. Kokopiness found a nook at the back of the hall where he installed himself, he hoped invisibly.

According to their custom, before the meeting, the chief and Councillors circulated among the petitioners to ascertain the nature and the urgency of their requests. Kokopiness denied that his petition was important. It could be brought up later, when, he hoped privately, not so many people were about.

Kokopiness wanted heartily to go home. He did not want to state publicly that he needed relief. It was too much like begging, but worse, it reflected on his resourcefulness and his ability as a farmer to provide for his family. He resigned himself to suffering.

First he had to suffer through the interminable Council meeting, which began slowly under the direction of the Indian Agent. The Council had a long agenda. Gravelling the road, keeping delinquents off the road, appointing a road foreman and, finally, controlling bootleggers, were all on the list. Discussion about these matters took all morning. Long before the meeting was adjourned for lunch, Kokopiness was bored.

In the afternoon, other things were considered; sending a delegate to a conference, admitting illegitimate children to band membership, which inspired fierce debate, setting quotas for the cutting of pine, which inspired only mild debate, and controlling cattle and dogs. Fierce argument did not hasten the meeting. The more heated the debate the longer the meeting became. The Agent suggested that other matters be dealt with after supper, and once more the meeting was adjourned to resume at 7.00 PM.

The evening portion of the Council meeting was set aside for considering petitions and other matters brought to the Council by members of the band. There were requests for permits of various kinds, leases of land, and enfranchisements. By this time, Kokopiness had begun easing his boredom by intermittent naps, rousing from time to time as the meeting droned on. Long speeches had a soporific effect on Kokopiness that even the depleted state of his larder and his reluctance to reveal his problem could not overcome.

Each time he awoke, he looked around, and, satisfied that the audience was still too large to allow him to present his request, went back to dozing...

Kokopiness woke up slowly. A Council member was speaking.

"I heard not long ago... that days... nights... in China ... when it's day... Canada it's night... earth turns... "

Kokopiness shook his head.

"Yeah, and we're upside down at night and rightside up during the day," explained a learned Councillor to his disbelieving colleagues.

Kokopiness got up.

The chief saw Kokopiness standing.

"Is there anything you'd like to ask?" the chairman inquired.

"No," replied Kokopiness putting on his cap. He went out the door.

The chief and his Council were puzzled.

Kokopiness whistling, hurried home through the night. He was very pleased.

The house was dark when he arrived. Everyone was sleeping. He went upstairs.

"Hey Maugneet!" Kokopiness said to his wife shaking her shoulder so violently he knocked off her tam.

"What?" Margaret grumbled at the onslaught.

"I jus' learned where the potatoes went. The eart' turns. At night we're upside down. Them potatoes musta fall outa the pit," said Kokopiness in excitement.

Margaret sat bolt upright in her bed, and slammed her tam back on her head. "You damn fool. Get the hell outa here and get that money. I don't give a damn if we're upside down and the potatoes fell out. If we don't get that money we're going to be hungry."

She pushed Kokopiness down the stairs and out of the door. "Go and get that money," she insisted to his retreating back.

Kokopiness made his painful way back to the Council Hall, wondering why he, unlike the potatoes did not fall off the face of the earth.

The Council Hall was dark and silent when he arrived. Kokopiness scratched his head. Now what?

In a Pig's Eye

Old John Zhawshaw (Swallow) was an inveterate traveller and incomparable *raconteur*. In all probability he developed his disposition to see the world simply to avoid work. What he gained through travel, Old John shared with the people of Moose Meat Point. It was through John that the Ojibway of that reserve came to know about events elsewhere and many aspects of technical progress.

By his own accounts, Old John had slept with the Seminoles in Florida, ate with the Cherokee in Oklahoma, danced with the Sioux in Minnesota, and drank with the Catawba in South Carolina. He described Chinese and East Indians and other exotic peoples. He told about the Civil War and the Battle of Little Big Horn.

He brought news of airplanes, cars, telephones, electric lights, and cameras. His compatriots, incredulous, doubted him, but he seemed cheerfully indifferent.

Old John was gone frequently from the reserve, often remaining away from home for periods varying from a couple of months to three years or more. But he always returned with new and startling revelations about the ingenuity of the white man and his world.

He had come back to Moose Meat Point one autumn after a lengthy absence. Where he had been, no one knew or really cared.

On his return, hog-killing time was in full swing. To earn some money for himself, and to acquire some pork for the winter, Old John assisted at hog slaughters.

Old John was critical of the hog-killing techniques of his

Moose Meat Point compatriots, but not openly. There was neither much polish nor economy in their executions. A trough and a hot meal of mash were all that were used to lure a pig to the executioner and his knife. A swift incision, a little time, and the victim would collapse lifeless, bloody, and senseless on the ground. Simple and effective, yet in Old John's view, wasteful and unrefined.

At first, Old John said nothing about his contempt of such old-fashioned methods. But always talkative, he eventually disclosed to Shigun (Bass) that there were better ways of hog-killing devised by the clever white man.

"John, you kill my pig, you?"

"Yeah, shore," Old John assured confidently.

"John! How dem white peoples kill pig?" Shigun asked.

"First you make good fire an' boil water in barr'l.

"Den you get pig, tie his back feet and hang him upside down from limb of tree." Shigun listened with fascination as John, himself enraptured by his knowledge, continued: "Den put tub under pig. Den cut pig's neck. All blood fall into tub. Very easy."

"What, keep blood for?" Shigun asked.

"For make blood sausage; good for to eat," Old John said.

"Don't t'ink, need blood, me," Shigun broke in, shaking his head.

"Den I take blood. Make good sausage, me." Old John brightened up and spit out a stream of tobacco juice.

"Mebbe, you wan' keep head, for make cheese?" Old John inquired. "Tas'e real good," and he almost smacked his lips.

"Don' wan' head eider," Shigun refused, his brow knitting. "Never heard of dat, me."

"Den I keep head. Okay?" John asked. Shigun nodded.

"How about feet. Wannah keep dem? Dey good for pickling." John asked again.

"No, don' wan' dem, me. Just wan meat; good meat." Shigun emphasized, his tone rasping. "You can keep all dem t'ings, and de tail too, if you wan'."

"Don' know what you missing you," John commented sadly. "Tail make good soup. Mebee if Indians aroun' here don' wan' dose t'ings, I can take dem. Have good winter, me. Won' hab to work." John mused out loud and hopefully. "Hey! Shigun can I hab de guts?" Old John blurted out.

"Yeah. You can hab dem. What you wan' dem for?" Shigun wanted to know.

"For wrapping sausages and weiner. Keep longer dat way," Old John replied.

By this time, Shigun was uneasy that he had asked Old John to officiate at the slaying of his pig, a beast of some three or four hundred pounds.

"Don't keep ME no guts," he said with shuddering assurance.

"Won't matter," declared Old John. "I take dem an' anything else you don' wan'."

"Kill the pig tomorrow, you?" inquired Shigun anxious to see the results of John's revelations, and wanting to get his winter supply of meat processed for storage.

"Don' tink so, me. We need horse, pulley, big string, maybe hunerd feet, steel bar'l, and some scrapers, and bags. Take coupla days maybe to get all dat stuff."

"Scrapers?" inquired Shigun, with eyebrows threatening to disappear under his cap. "What for?"

"Oh, yeah," explained Old John. "For combing off pig hair. You can sell hair. White man use hair for hair brushes and tooth brushes."

Shigun winced at Old John's disclosure. He was glad he was Indian. He watched the object of the preparations lounging in a satisfying wallow of mud, wondering why anyone would think to use bristles, so exposed, on his head or in his mouth. Secretly he wondered what "in a pig's eye" meant, but he did not ask.

Shigun's interest in killing the pig in the newest mode began to wane. Such a simple operation was becoming too complex, and he began to wish that he had not asked Old John to assist. But it was too late now. Moreover, the desire to be first, even in hog-killing, was too compelling.

Next day Shigun borrowed a neighbour's horse. With the creature he went to Blunder Bay and bought a pulley on credit. On the way back, he borrowed a hundred-foot rope from a prosperous white farmer, and secured a steel barrel from the local minister. At the same time, he invited several people to take part in the ceremony the following day.

Preparations commenced early the succeeding day with the kindling of a forceful fire beneath the steel barrel, which had been filled with water. People began to arrive. They watched in amazement at the suspension of a pulley from the large arm of an elm, and the insertion of the rope through the eye of the block.

Near the fire, on a table, a fearsome variety of instruments were displayed, glinting in the sunlight. There were knives of different sizes, an axe, a hack-saw, an ordinary saw, a mallet, files, scrapers, and strings. Under the elm grazed the horse.

The Indians, having inspected the almost surgical array of instruments, retired to the shade of another tree to await the spectacle.

Old John was at his calm, cheerful best when talking to neighbours.

"Ready?" the owner of the pig shouted to Old John.

"Water boiling?" countered the butcher.

"Yeah," the terse answer came back.

"Okay, get de pig," agreed Old John.

The proprietor of the pig hurried off. He returned in a few minutes, followed willingly by his property, who was nipping away at several cobs of corn, held loosely in Shigun's right hand. Shigun dropped the cobs on the grass directly beneath the dangling rope. The pig happily devoured his last meal. While the pig was preoccupied, Shigun and his assistant, under the direction of John Zhawshaw tied the back legs of the pig. The pig uncurled and swished his tail.

"Giddap," ordered the teamster, after receiving the nod from Old John.

"Whoa!" The horse stopped. The rope had tightened and the pig lurched into the air upside down. In the process he had lost his cob and was squealing.

An assistant quickly placed a twenty inch length of board between the pig's ankles, which added to the pig's offended clamour. The spectators were quizzical. Old John nodded to the driver.

"Giddap," came the order.

As commanded the horse strained forward. The pig rose ponderously into the air, swinging, swaying, and complaining, his snout flushed.

"A liddle more, dere," shouted John.

"Giddap," came the command.

"Whoa!" called out John as the pig's blushing head rose to the four-foot level.

"Whoa! Whoa! Whoa!" came the chorus of executioner's assistants, to make sure that the horse heard, and understood.

The horse, nobody's fool, demonstrated his excellent hearing by stopping at once.

Everyone moved into action quietly and swiftly. Old John took the knife; Shigun clasped the pig's right front leg to hold him steady, an assistant deposited a tub beneath the pig. The pig's squeals of outrage increased as he bobbed gently up and down The spectators were impressed with the precision of the work—like clockwork—just like the white man!

There was a creaking grumble from above, followed by an ear-rending crack. The executioner and his assistants dove for safety, just in time, as the branch of the elm tore loose from the tree. The jagged, slivered limb struck the horse smartly on the rump.

The horse bolted straight for the bushes on the other side of the field, dragging the pig, whose squeals had reached a crescendo, in a cloud of dust behind him. Behind the horse and the pig ran eight or nine dogs barking at the new form of sport, followed closely by Shigun, cursing horse, pig, dogs, assistants, executioner, and all new inventions. Last in line ran twenty or so Indians, howling with laughter.

You Can Have Her: I Don't Want Her

It was a hot day, fit more for leisure than for work. Both Captain and Low Down, young men in their late teens, were lounging on the verandah of the village general store enjoying their leisure, a product of involuntary, but not unwelcome unemployment.

At noon, the traffic in and out of the store increased. Parents entered the store with their children in little flocks behind them; and emerged with potato sacks bulging with groceries while the children clutched moisture-frosted bottles of pop or cones of ice-cream that dripped cool sweetness over their brown, chubby fingers, defying their busy tongues. Captain swallowed; Low Down licked his lips.

"Musta got that on credit," complained Captain enviously, as one family, burdened with packages, and children dripping strawberry globules filed out of the store and trudged up the road.

"Yeah!" agreed Low Down languidly as he lay back beside Captain on the rough planking of the verandah with his fingers interlaced behind his head. He closed his eyes against the glare of the sun and to spare his stomach the sight of such unbearable goodness. He composed himself for sleep.

"Hi Captain! Hi Low Down!"

Captain and Low Down opened their eyes.

"Hi Bertha!" they shouted in sudden and enthusiastic unison to Bertha, better known as Power Pack for her friendly disposition.

Captain and Low Down watched her well-rounded posterior undulate down the road toward the Indian Agent's corner. Inspired by her grace, they forgot their hunger.

Once more they lapsed in drowsiness and lethargy. It was much too warm for sustained effort. Neither spoke for some time.

"It'd be kinda nice to go to the dance in Onion Valley Friday night," observed Low Down nonchalantly to a passing cloud.

"Yeah!" Captain agreed diffidently to the same cloud. He knew what Low Down was thinking. He himself had been moved by Power Pack's beauty and was touched by the fact that she had spoken to him first, recognizing his superiority. But he did not trust Low Down. Long association had confirmed that there was no wisdom in accepting Low Down's suggestions, or even his innocent remarks without considering them carefully.

Low Down was not disturbed because Power Pack had named him after greeting Captain. Obviously she was a discriminating young lady who kept the best for last. Secure in the knowledge of his own superiority, Low Down was thinking fast.

"First one to think of a job that gets us work gets Power Pack. O.K.?" Low Down proposed after some deliberation.

"Okay," Captain concurred. "Cheez, you'd do anything for love. Eh, Low Down?"

Low Down grinned at the compliment to his virility. "Shake," he said, and offered his hand to Captain, who took it as a solemn seal of the agreement between them for Power Pack's companionship.

But there was a dearth of possible employers.

"How about the minister?" suggested Low Down.

"Naw. He never gives nothing, only takes," Captain reflected. "Same thing with the priest."

Similarly Captain rejected all the names proposed by Low Down.

"Why don't YOU think of someone then?" asked Low Down exasperated with Captain's negative attitude.

Captain frowned, knitted his brow in hard, laborious thought.

"Hey'" said Captain brightening and jumping to his feet. "My uncle! Come on!" and he turned without waiting for agreement.

Low Down jumped up and trotted off after Captain.

It took very little time to walk to the house of Captain's uncle, which was situated down the road and over a small rise which blocked it from sight on the store verandah. By the time they arrived, both boys were perspiring freely.

They walked into the house wiping their foreheads with their sleeves. Without preamble Captain came straight to the point. He was like that–direct–seldom beating around the bush.

"Hey, Uncle John, me and Low Down need a job. We're broke. How about letting us help you?"

"On a day like this?" Uncle commented stoking his pipe with a match. Young people were a source of astonishment to him.

"Yeah," insisted Captain.

"Got mosta my hay cut. Don't need any more. Gonna be a couple days before it needs coiling," replied Uncle John.

But Captain saw an opening here. "If we cut some more hay for you, you could sell it."

"Don't think so," said John. "Don't trust you guys anyway. Might play and break something."

Captain felt his uncle weakening; he was not objecting to the idea of work.

"Come on Uncle. I promise we won't play. You got that field up at prairie cut yet? Hell, bet me and Low Down can cut that fifteen acres by tonight. Ain't that right, Low Down?"

"Sure, Captain. Nothing to it."

"I dunno, Captain," replied the old man weakening. "I'd like to, but my team is kinda new, ain't broke in good yet. Kinda wild. Don't think you can handle them."

"Hell, Uncle. You know Low Down here. Ain't a horse he can't handle. His father used to keep horses so he's got all kinds of experience. Ain't that right Low Down?"

"That's right Captain," Low Down confirmed smugly.

"How much?" asked Uncle John, narrowing his eyes, ready for a haggle. He sensed a shrewd bargain could be made.

"Ten dollars," Captain said quickly.

"That's too much for a couple of guys with no experience," muttered John shaking his head.

"Seven dollars. And we rake and coil the hay too in a coupla days. O.K., Captain?" Low Down believed in collective bargaining.

"Guess so!" Captain mumbled, casting dark looks at Low Down. Some bargain HE drove.

John got up beaming. "It's a deal! You cut the hay, and rake and coil it when it's ready. Mower's up at the field already. I'll hitch up the horses for you. Just remember, don't let go of them lines. Keep a good holt on 'em all the time, and be careful with them horses. Come on. I'll pay you five dollars tonight and the rest when you finish."

John, with Captain and Low Down in tow went out to the barn to hitch up the horses. Within ten minutes, the horses were hitched to a wagon equipped with hay racks fore and aft.

Nimble Captain leaped on the wagon and took the reins from his uncle. Low Down jumped up beside him.

"Giddap!" shouted the boys in unison, and they were underway.

"Watch out for them horses," shouted John with a wave. "Give dem a drink at the lake."

"Okay!" the boys agreed as Captain guided the horses to the left at the road and headed in the direction of the store. Low Down clutched at the wagon for support.

"Guess I get Power Pack," chortled Captain over the rumble of the wheels on the stones.

Low Down said nothing. He was happy enough with the prospect of making some money. Anyway, he reflected, girls were a dime a dozen around Onion Valley. Might pick up a white girl even. Low Down imagined the look that would come over Captain's face in that event, and grinned. Life was good!

At the store corner, Captain again made a left turn down toward the Indian Agent's corner and the bay. The distance was short, consequently it did not take the team long to trudge down to the great stone mansion in which the Indian Agent was installed, and which had become the place to go when one wished to sit awhile and talk to friends.

As they passed in front of the agent's residence, Captain and Low Down were hailed by a group of ladies of assorted sizes, shapes and ages who were sitting on chairs and benches within the shaded verandah. All the ladies had their stockings rolled below the knees against the heat, some had gone so far as to roll them down to the ankle for comfort's sake. All fanned themselves with newspapers and occasionally used their aprons to wipe the moisture from their brows.

"'Lo boys," they shouted. "Ain't it a scorcher?"

Captain and Low Down cheerfully confirmed that it was indeed "a real hot day." They waved at the ladies.

The horses needed no urging to head straight for the beach and into the shallow bay until the water reached their knees. They drank, edging out further until the water reached their bellies.

"I'm going for a swim," Captain announced as he shed his

clothing. "You hold on to the reins while I go in, 'n then I'll hold them for you. Don't let go, like Uncle John says." Captain handed the reins to Low Down.

Captain clambered up the rear rack, perched for a moment on the top rung before diving in.

"Chump," he hit the water in a shallow dive. His stern disappeared into the waves.

The noise startled the horses who whinnied and started. Low Down soothed them. "Whoa Nellie! Whoa Queenie!"

Captain's head broke through the surface some distance from the horses, who still rolled their eyes in fright. He shouted exultantly, "Ever good." He swam back to the wagon and pulled himself on board.

"Your turn," he sputtered.

Low Down needed no further encouragement. He surrendered the reins to Captain and peeled off his clothing. He, too, climbed the rack and crouched for a moment before diving like a kingfisher into the inviting blueness below.

"Kachump," the horses shivered at this noise; again snorted and whickered.

"Easy there girls. Easy," soothed Captain.

Low Down burst to the surface, puffing and snorting, then swam back to the wagon grinning. "Ever nice!" he agreed.

Captain plunged in while Low Down waited. When Captain returned, Low Down dove in. And so it went, each boy taking a turn. Never had it been so abundantly good to swim.

"Last dive," said Captain hurling himself into the water. He dove as far as his lungs would take him. Captain surfaced, drew in a long breath, and tossed back his hair so that water would not drip in his eyes. Something clutched at his foot; Low Down surfaced right beside him.

With a laugh Captain shoved him down again. When he surfaced, both boys laughed.

"My God! The horses! You left the horses!"

Captain shouted accusingly at Low Down. The horses were already half-way to shore, plunging and snorting, the wagon wheels churning up the water in sprays.

Captain and Low Down gave chase as fast as the chest deep water would allow, half running, half swimming. By the time they had reached water that was shallow enough to permit them to run more freely, the horses and the wagon were past the Indian Agent's Office, clattering damply in the direction of home, amid a cloud of dust. Tied like flags to the racks fluttered the pants and shirts the boys had removed for their swim.

Captain and Low Down sprinted after the fleeing team. Gaining the shore, they raced up the incline.

On the Indian Agent's verandah a variety of gasps were heard from the assembled ladies.

"Shame! Vulgar! Awful! Disgraceful! Scandalous! Dear Lord!" wailed the ladies in horror. They arose in a body and began to file into the house. None could resist one last look at the amazing sight.

"Stark naked!" cried one, covering her eyes with her hands, but parting her fingers slightly to check to see if her eyes had deceived her first impression. They had not.

"Broad daylight, and no clothes!" moaned another, as she, too, took one last look before she entered the house.

One aged crone giggled lewdly all the way to the door, which she refused to enter without a great deal of encouragement from the others.

Captain and Low Down came to an abrupt halt. Indeed they were naked, a fact that had not occurred to them before, in their haste to recapture the horses.

And there was Power Pack hugging the Agent's mailbox, rocking with laughter.

"You guys miss the wagon train?" she guffawed. "It went by a minute ago."

Captain and Low Down tried ineffectively to cover certain portions of their bodies which might embarrass a young lady of Power Pack's temperament. Too late. Power Pack regarded this fresh evidence of modesty, hung limply to the mailbox, and went into fresh gales of laughter. The boys cast a final panic-stricken look at the disappearing team, now careening around the store corner and picking up speed. Captain and Low Down raced back to the beach, and into the water where they waded up to their chests, neither saying anything. After all, what was there to say?

"What now?" Low Down inquired plaintively.

Captain knitted his brow. He thought; he could always think in situations like this.

"Hey, Low Down," Captain asked hopefully, "Does your father keep oilers in his boat?"

"Yeah, I think so," said Low Down uncertainly.

"Let's go!" said the decisive Captain, and both waded over to the creek mouth where Low Down's father kept his boat moored.

"By God, they're here," said Captain snatching the pants from the bottom of the boat.

"They're MY dad's," snarled Low Down jerking them from Captain's hands. "You get the coat."

Captain did not argue. He took the coat, glad enough to have covering for his nakedness. The coat was redolent of reeking fish; still he put it on. It covered him to his kneecaps, his hands lost in the folds of the sleeves. Low Down was more than amply covered by the pants which reached his armpits. He grasped them with his hands and with his elbows. There was no belt.

"Cheez, they stink!" Captain commented wrinkling up his nose.

They walked up the incline. Low Down grinned. Power Pack was still standing by the mailbox.

"Oh, no! Not her again!" exclaimed Captain.

But Captain and Low Down could not avoid her.

"Dressed for the dance?" roared Power Pack, and burst out laughing once more.

The boys stalked past her with as much dignity as they could muster. "Oh, shut up!" Captain snarled, clutching a coat that threatened to come open. He reddened.

"You can have her, I don't want her," hummed Low Down as they passed her by.

PART 2

CHRISTIANITY, RELIGION AND WORSHIP AT MOOSE MEAT POINT

The Miracle

The old lady wanted to smoke. She had not had a puff for several days because her clay pipe was broken. She was not a heavy smoker by any means, but she enjoyed a nightly pipeful. Though she had an ample supply of shag tobacco and snuff, there was no way she could satisfy her desire for a smoke without a pipe.

When her grandson, Rufus, about age eight, accompanied by his friend Fred, an eleven year old grade four boy, came home from school, the old lady asked them to go to the general store to buy a new pipe. As a reward she would give each of them a penny for their errand. And she handed Fred, the older boy, five pennies.

"Now, don't play along the way. Come straight home, you can play afterwards."

Rufus and Fred shot out the door and dashed down the dirt road toward the store one bended mile away. With such dispatch, it did not take them long to arrive at the store, where Fred stated the purpose of their call.

"Rufus' grandmother sent us to buy a new pipe; she broke her old pipe," Fred explained.

"You got five cents?" the storekeeper inquired.

"Yeah!" Fred shot back, extending an open hand toward the storekeeper. The storekeeper took the pennies, counted them twice, before depositing them in a cardboard shoe box. He then rummaged around in some drawers, selected a white short-stemmed clay pipe which he put in a small brown paper bag.

Fred took the bag from the storekeeper. He and Rufus cheerfully started for home, Fred carrying the precious package delicately, Rufus trotting close by his side.

About half-way home, Rufus turned to his friend, and informed Fred, "My turn to carry the pipe."

"You're too small," Fred refused looking down at Rufus.

"But the pipe is not heavy, and I'm strong enough!" Rufus argued casting his eyes upon the bag.

"No. You might drop it and break it." Fred explained, sniffing and clutching the brown paper bag a little tighter.

"But I won't break it, I'll be real careful," Rufus pleaded still eyeing the bag.

"You might trip or something," Fred haughtily stated.

"But it's *my* grandmother's pipe." Rufus reasoned breathing a little harder and drawing still closer to Fred's side.

"No!" was all Fred uttered with a sniff of finality.

Little Rufus was burning. He had been adjudged too small, weak, careless, and clumsy. His pleas had been ignored as worthless.

Small as he was, Rufus was as determined to carry the pipe as his friend Fred was scrupulous to duty. Rufus reasoned that he was entitled to carry the pipe because in the first place it belonged to his grandmother; in the second place, the money expended in the purchase of the pipe came from his grandmother's purse; and in the last place, it was unfair of Fred to deny him some honour in bearing the pipe home. Rufus was burning; he was seething but he said nothing more, walking quietly beside his friend.

Suddenly, Rufus made a grab for the brown paper bag. While he was unable to take full and complete possession of the prized package, Rufus succeeded in knocking the bag from Fred's strong grasp. The bag fell to the ground. Fred pounced upon it; Rufus flung himself upon Fred.

They struggled. Rufus, the aggressor, put his arms around Fred's neck which he twisted this way and that, shouting "Gimmee the bag; gimmee the bag." Fred, the custodian, doubled over clutching the bag to his bosom, unable to retaliate, and yelled frantically, "Don't, don't." Rufus ignored him. He began pummelling Fred's head with his fists.

"It's broken!" Fred gasped. Rufus, startled, abandoned his assault upon Fred. Dusting himself off slightly he knelt beside Fred and watched as his friend opened the crumpled and now tattered bag. Fred reached into the bag and drew out two pieces, the bowl and the stem. The pipe had broken at the base. Rufus, eyes round, looked at Fred in dismay.

"It's all your fault," Fred, glaring, accused the frightened Rufus.

"What will we do?" asked Rufus.

Fred said nothing, but he looked worried and trembled as he sorrowfully and without real conviction went through the motions of fitting the stem to the bowl. Rufus looked on not really expecting the broken pipe to join of its own accord. Rufus, then only in Grade One, could think of nothing except the swift and certain punishment that he was sure to receive on arrival home.

"Maybe we can get some glue, or borrow or steal a pipe," Rufus proposed brightly.

Fred said nothing. He only continued to gaze at the pipe; he was preoccupied with the exercise of fitting the broken pieces together.

"We're going to pray for a miracle," he announced.

Rufus was startled. He had not yet been exposed to much religion or other learning but he knew what prayers were. Of miracles or their nature, he was absolutely ignorant.

"What's a miracle?" Rufus asked in a sort of bewildered way, not understanding the term "miracle" in either English or Ojibway.

Manfully Fred tried to explain in Ojibway what miracle meant. He stumbled, "It's doing something strange, like healing the pipe until its just like new; like its never been broken."

"Where'd you learn that?" Rufus inquired his eyes narrowing.

"In the Bible," Fred said matter of factly.

"Did they heal pipes?" Rufus asked amazed.

"No, but they did other things," Fred muttered while he swept sand into a pile.

"What other things?" Rufus wanted to know.

"Well, Jesus multiplied bread and fishes." Fred said, sweeping sand with his hands.

Rufus, his knowledge of English and scriptures severely limited, did not understand.

"What's bread; what's multiplication?" he pressed.

"Bread is like bannock; only white people eat it," Fred explained, "and multiplication is making more."

"My grandmother can always make more, and that's not . . . what you call it, a miracle," Rufus said.

Fred was exasperated; he stopped sweeping sand. "Listen," he told Rufus. "There was lots of people one time in one place. They was hungry. They had nothing to eat. One man had only five bannocks and maybe five trouts. Jesus prayed and took those five bannocks and five trouts and fed all the people. That's a miracle."

"What else did they do?" Rufus was getting interested in the Bible, forgetting the pipe.

"Another time, there was a big party. People got married. They ran out of wine. Jesus prayed and took water an' made it into wine," Fred interpreted the Bible.

"That's not healing, though," Rufus interjected, remembering the sick pipe, and still very doubtful. Fred sensed his little friend's lack of faith.

"Well. There was another time. A man was dead. He was buried. And Jesus prayed or something, and he told that man, Lazarus, to come out. An' Lazarus came out of the grave." Fred looked straight into Rufus' disbelieving and frightened eyes. "Jesus made that man come back to life," Fred whispered in awe.

After this short lesson from a Grade Four theologian, Rufus was prepared to pray for and engage in the enactment of a miracle. At the same time he began to admire and fear his older friend.

"I'll help you pray for a miracle," Rufus volunteered.

Fred who knew about such matters took charge.

"We'll have to make an altar first," he said as he resumed piling sand in the middle of the road. "Come on, help me." Rufus needed no urging. In a short while, the boys had a large sand pyramid.

Fred who was privy to the conduct of rituals, conducted the ceremony. Before starting, he placed the pipe on top of the sand altar with the stem meticulously fitted into the base of the bowl at the point of fracture, so that the junction would occur easily and naturally. Rufus was dazzled.

With the pipe in place, Fred instructed Rufus in the proper manner of inducing miracles. "Kneel down; join your hands; close your eyes; look up to heaven; and pray all your might to God. You must think only of the healing of the pipe. Do you understand?"

Rufus nodded; he understood. He dared not cross Fred. He was glad; it was all so simple.

"Say the 'Our Father,' with me, " Fred commanded, "Our Father, who art in heaven, hallowed be Thy Name . . . " Rufus, removing his eyes from heaven, looked down at the pipe, anxious to witness the actual miracle of junction take place. He bent forward for closer scrutiny and as he did so, forgot to continue repeating the words for the miracle. Fred, master of ceremonies, immediately noticed the expiry of Rufus' invocation. He opened his own eyes and saw his companion looking sacrilegiously at the impaired pipe.

Fred, in a righteous rage, seized Rufus by the lapels of his shirt collar and shook him.

For was Rufus not actually preventing a miracle? Was he not aborting the power of prayer? Fred glowered at Rufus.

"You're not supposed to look during miracles. You've got to keep your eyes closed. You've got to pray. You've got to think of God and the miracle. Didn't I tell you? Don't you understand? Do you want the pipe fixed?" Fred snorted and snarled out the sentences, all the while vigorously shaking Rufus, whose head jerked back and forth violently. Rufus nodded; he understood. Fred gave him another hair-waving shake.

"Don't you look again; If you look, the miracle won't happen, and it will be all your fault. If you look before we finish, I'm not going to help you; you can go home alone," Fred threatened. Rufus was frightened.

Fred resumed the petition, "In the name of the Father, The Son, The Holy Ghost. Amen. Our Father, who art in heaven, . . . " Fervently and holily, Rufus followed. At "lead us not into temptation" Rufus took a quick one-eyed peep at the most wondrous of acts.

He felt what seemed like a mighty blow accompanied by volcanic thunder and illuminated by blinding light. He saw a blue starless heaven, several moons and crooked wavering rainbows; he heard the buzz and drone of bees; he felt a tingle in his face. He could not think clearly. He could not see properly, especially when the trees on either side of the road were revolving. The sounds ceased; the tingling diminished; and gradually the trees began to stand still. He looked for Fred. But Fred was nowhere to be seen, nowhere to be heard. He called out Fred's name.

Rufus was horrified. "The miracle, the miracle" had taken his friend Fred. And he began to cry. Picking up the stem and bowl of the pipe, Rufus ran homeward in terror.

He ran into the house weeping and sniffling.

"What happened to you ?" his mother and grandmother asked simultaneously.

"The miracle, the miracle," he blurted out offering the broken pipe to his grandmother.

"What are you talking about? Look at you; you're all dirty

and dusty and your face and nose are all bloody. You must have been in a fight. You must have played along the way." Rufus' mother said going out the door.

"What happened?" his grandmother inquired.

Rufus told what he knew and what he could remember.

Rufus' mother came back in with a little stick. Brandishing the thin wand, she said: "This is a miracle. I'm going to give you a miracle."

Yellow Cloud's Battle with the Spirits

Decades ago the people of Moose Meat Point Indian Reserve began making weekly Saturday excursions into Blunder Bay, a distance of some twenty miles. The women went there to sell berries, quill-work, baskets and moccasins, and to purchase flour, lard, tea, salt pork and yarn; the men, to exchange furs, axe handles and other hardware for tobacco, nets, guns and shot. At the end of the day the Moose Meaters made their way home either on foot or by canoe. A few lingered behind to do business with some Blunder Bay bootlegger.

While most people had gone into Blunder Bay at some time or other, there were some who simply had no interest, desire or reason to go into town. Yellow Cloud, an older man of sixty or so, was one of those who had never gone to town. Besides having no inclination to go to Blunder Bay, old Yellow Cloud did not speak English. And being a bashful type he did not wish embarrassment at the hands of white people. The best way to avoid contact with the whites was by staying away from them and their towns.

Frankly, though, he was afraid that he might be arrested for an assault that he had perpetrated one day on a white man who had come to purchase axe handles from him. Yellow Cloud's wife, his interpreter, was away on the afternoon of that fateful day when the white man arrived and began inquiring about Alexander. At least that was the only word that Yellow Cloud extracted from the torrent of gibberish that he heard but could not understand. He, in turn, speaking in Ojibway tried as best as he could to direct the white man to Alexander's home which was just down the road. The white man refused to leave.

They began shouting at one another. When the white man, pointing to the pile of axe handles which were lying neatly near the door, actually reached for one, Yellow Cloud clouted him with an axe handle that he had been fashioning. The white man dazed from the blow and bleeding from a gash on his head staggered out the house and ran down the path a ways before stopping to wave his fist and shout imprecations at Yellow Cloud. Even though Yellow Cloud could not understand English, he could deduce from the gesticulations and the tone that he was being cursed; and even though this incident had occurred years before, the curse had never been lifted. The white man had never come back to forgive him. Yellow Cloud was certain that his victim would sooner or later seek revenge. As long as he remained within the confines of the reserve, Yellow Cloud felt safe.

Lately, having been converted to Christianity, Yellow Cloud was beginning to lose some of his apprehensions and at the same time to acquire some degree of confidence.

Part of the religious instructions that he received consisted of purging old superstitions. Old Yellow Cloud was assured that he had nothing to fear from Weendigo, the evil being who devoured those guilty of any form of excess. Yellow Cloud was also guaranteed that "Maeko-bimossae," the dreaded monster, did not exist. No person possessed the power of transforming himself into any animal form, be it bear, owl, dog, or snake in order to inflict harm or death or disease upon another. In addition, Yellow Cloud was to renounce idolatrous beliefs in personal patrons, the incorporeal essence of all beings, and the primacy of plants and animals. Moreover, he was to abjure medicine men and all Indian ceremonies.

Having embraced such beliefs and taken part in the ceremonies for sixty years or more, Yellow Cloud found it difficult to abandon them. Even more difficult was the espousal of new beliefs and attendance at new ceremonies. Accepting the Ten Commandments was easy enough, but trusting in angels, saints, and guardians was, he felt, not much different from invoking his own traditional patrons. He became a Christian in name but not in conviction.

In fact, old Yellow Cloud was confused, and in his confusion he became a skeptic believing in neither his tribe's beliefs nor the tenets of Christianity.

He even questioned what he was told. He scoffed at reports of the telegraph; ridiculed the idea of wheeled vehicles that moved of their own accord; and scorned the notion of canoes that could be propelled without paddles. "That can't be," he said. "Whoever heard of such things?"

The only thing that he believed in was the efficacy of prayer. Since prayer was the only practice that was not proscribed in either English or Ojibway, Yellow Cloud prayed. If praying did nothing else, it at least comforted him.

Eventually Yellow Cloud's wife persuaded him to go into Blunder Bay. She said that it would be like a holiday for him and that he should see some of the marvellous attainments of the clever white man before he died. Yellow Cloud did not really want to go, nor was he near death, but to please his wife and to satisfy his own curiosity he finally consented.

When Yellow Cloud reluctantly decided to go into Blunder Bay, his wife was unable to accompany him because she was feeling somewhat unwell. Nct wishing to go alone or to paddle all the way, he went with a friend Kukijeesh (Ground Hog) who had a horse and a buggy. It was a little faster that way, and the journey afforded Yellow Cloud a chance to know the road.

Yellow Cloud and his friend set out early and arrived just before noon at an inn in the outskirts of Blunder Bay down by the lake. There were a large number of Moose Meaters lounging on the grounds already and many more at the shore, arriving both by canoe and by wagon. Yellow Cloud's friend hitched the horse to a tree midst greetings from their relatives and acquaintances.

"First time in town, eh, Yellow Cloud," one commented in Ojibway.

"Yep!" Yellow Cloud muttered.

"Must be very special occasion," another observed.

"Nothing special, just came," Yellow Cloud answered.

"You should have brought your axe handles," still another acquaintance offered. "You could'a sold lots. Better still you could'a clubbed a few white men. Lotsa them around. Haw, haw, haw."

Yellow Cloud winced. He had almost forgotten about the incident that had occurred a few years previously. Obviously others had not. If others could still remember the event, most assuredly his victim would remember it.

"Come on, let's go," Yellow Cloud's friend urged cheerfully.

"I think I'll stay here," Yellow Cloud sputtered, looking around to see if there were any white men.

"What's the matter?" Kukijeesh wanted to know.

"Nothing. I'll stay here for a while. I'll look after the horse. You can go. I'll go later." Yellow Cloud assured his friend.

As Kukijeesh turned to go, Yellow Cloud shouted at him "When are we going home?"

"About six or seven this evening. We'll meet here," Yellow Cloud's friend shouted back.

Yellow Cloud sat down on the grass. He pulled his coat collar up around his ears, readjusted his cap, and hunched his shoulders before leaning back against the tree. He hoped no white man would come down to the shore. He now regretted that he had come into town. There was nothing to do. He could have remained on the reserve hunting, fishing or doing something. But here he was with nothing to do; worse still, he was vulnerable. If the Blunder Bay people knew he was in town, they would certainly inform his victim and the police of his presence. Never know what would happen, but he could guess.

Yellow Cloud shivered as he felt a chill. He knew it would be unwise to attempt escape, especially in broad daylight. He would be seen. Staying where he sat was hardly better, particularly with Moose Meaters around. Not only were they abundantly friendly and affectionate that day, but they were also enthusiastically and loudly proclaiming their love for him as well as announcing his presence. Never had he been greeted so often or so energetically.

"Yellow Cloud! How are you?" was repeated many times.

"Yellow Cloud!" His name resounded along the shore.

The old man wished the people were less friendly; they were almost as bad as enemies. There was nothing he could do; he was helpless.

Then Yellow Cloud remembered the missionary's guidance. When beset by troubles, pray. Yellow Cloud, besieged by a pile of trouble, began to pray. He petitioned heaven with all the fervour that he could muster to forestall white people coming to the beach; he entreated the archangels for their guardianship; and, he beseeched the heavenly host for his protection and safe journey back to the reserve.

The afternoon wore on. Yellow Cloud remained undiscovered although his name was invoked repeatedly and clamorously. No white men, as far as he could see, were summoned by the proclamation of their names. His fear began to wane; maybe he would escape; maybe prayer would obtain his release from his predicament.

Evening came. The Moose Meaters started to leave for

home. Like the others, he wanted to get home to eat and rest. Sitting there underneath the tree, as he had all afternoon, had made him tired and hungry. It was worse than working all day. As much as he wanted, he could not go home without Kukijeesh. Nor could he take the horse and buggy without permission. Yellow Cloud had to wait. Had he not given his word? And the longer he remained the greater the chances of getting caught. He was glad it was getting dark. At least he could now stand up and move about.

Yellow Cloud sauntered over to join a small group of Moose Meaters who were standing around a small bonfire that they had lit for their evening meal. He gratefully accepted a cup of tea.

He was not there very long when he and his friends heard the hooting and hollering and the raucous laughter of a party of men headed their way. Yellow Cloud recognized the voice of his friend and companion. He was glad; at last, he could go home.

The party arrived—five Moose Meaters and a white man. They drew up. Kukijeesh introduced the white man, a jelly-bellied, florid-faced, queezy-voiced individual.

"Dis is de man you hit wid axe handle," Kukijeesh slurred in Ojibway by way of introduction and he roared. Everyone else roared. Yellow Cloud looked up. He was horrified.

"Dis is de man dat hit you wid axe handle long time ago," Kukijeesh garbled before roaring again and clapping the white man's shoulder. And everyone else laughed too.

But Yellow Cloud was off. He did not wait to shake hands or to find out whether he had been forgiven. All he knew was that he had been discovered and could be arrested. He ran and ran. Old Yellow Cloud did not stop running, difficult as it was on the wagon trail ruts, until he was several miles from the scene of the meeting. Exhausted and gasping for breath, he collapsed on the side of the road where he lay for a long time before recovering sufficiently to sit up.

Too tired to continue, Yellow Cloud, made an overnight camp by constructing, a few yards from the main road, a small lean-to over a bedding of soft and fragrant cedar boughs. He prayed for his salvation and for his delivery from the clutches of the white man and then fell asleep, his hunger forgotten.

Some time later, Yellow Cloud was roused from his deep slumber by a rumbling sound. At first, he thought that he was dreaming. Pinching himself to make sure that it was neither dream nor imagination, Yellow Cloud raised his head and listened. There was no mistake. It was not a vain product of the imagination or an impalpable melody of fantasy. It was real and it was coming from the direction of Blunder Bay. Yellow Cloud was fully awake, every sense tingling with excitement and fever.

The roar was quite unlike anything that Yellow Cloud had ever heard. It was deeper than that of bear; more menacing than that of wolf; more insistent than that of dog. It was none of these; but whatever it was, it growled and roared continuously, drawing closer and closer. Yellow Cloud began to tremble.

He raised himself slowly from a reclining position, got to his feet, and stumbled toward the wagon trail. Yellow Cloud looked in the direction of town, from whence he had come. A quivering yellow glow of light wavered in the distance, growing brighter as it came nearer, a glow as yellow as the moon.

Yellow Cloud rubbed his eyes. No, he was not mistaken. He shivered and trembled before he realized that he was alarmed. "Maeko-bimossae," the dreaded Bearwalker! Yet it could not be. Though he had never seen nor encountered one before, he had heard that the evil monsters emitted a different glow which alternately went on and off much like a fire-fly. It was also said and confirmed by all those who had sighted or met Maeko-bimossae, that the fiend floated a few feet above the crowns of trees or above the ground in its passage toward its victim. Nor could Yellow Cloud remember from the accounts that he had heard of Maeko-bimossae that the monster growled or roared. All the logic and reason did not allay Yellow Cloud's growing apprehension as he continued to gaze in the direction of the glow and rumble.

As Yellow Cloud watched, a yellow ball of brilliant light appeared around the bend, about a mile down the wagon trail, bouncing and growling menacingly. It's light did not go out but shone strongly and directly upon Yellow Cloud. There was no doubt in Yellow Cloud's mind that it was the dreaded Maeko-bimossae, set upon him by the white man who certainly had just cause.

Yellow Cloud perspired, his legs shook, his arms trembled; he felt numb and cold all over. He began to pray "Our Father who art in heaven . . . Amen." Maeko-bimossae kept coming, roaring louder. "Our Father who art in heaven . . . Amen." Prayer was powerless, unable to repel Maeko-bimossae who kept snorting and shining harder. White man's prayer was in vain against an Indian monster.

What, he wondered, marked him out for such bad luck?

Was it because he had become Christian? No! It could not be; else he would have been harmed long since. Was it the white man who had hired an Indian medicine man to harm him? It must be. "Our Father who art in heaven . . . Amen" Louder this time. But the roar of Maeko-bimossae seemed to drown him out. Yellow Cloud's mind raced and reeled "Our Father who art in heaven . . . Amen." It was useless.

The hugest ball of brightest yellow light produced by the biggest of all Maeko-bimossae was shining directly upon him. Yellow Cloud could hardly see. Then suddenly the one brilliant ball mystically and inexplicably became two. Dread and terror gripped poor old Yellow Cloud. He was being attacked by two Maeko-bimossaes. There was no escape. The old man almost sank to his knees on the side of the roadway. He could stand behind a tree in the vain hope that the fiends would not detect him or leave him alone. He could put sand in his mouth, under his tongue. It was too late for that. There was only one thing to do. Stand up in front and face the monsters with raw courage.

The monsters, their yellow fiery eyes gleaming and voices roaring murderously were less than a hundred yards away. Yellow Cloud darted to the side of the road, seized a hefty stick, and dashed to the middle of the road. Heart pounding, hands trembling, cold perspiration dripping down his face, Yellow Cloud waited. The two roaring and growling monsters stopped a few feet in front of Yellow Cloud. He did not wait. Springing forward, Yellow Cloud raised his club and smashed the Maeko-bimossae on his right; he raised his club again, and slashed the other Maeko-bimossae with all his might and force.

"Hey! What the hell . . . " One of the monsters screamed in pain. Yellow Cloud dropped his club and ran in terror down the road. When he realized what he had done, Yellow Cloud slowed down. He had faced not one Maeko-bimossae, but two. He had stood up to them. He had killed them. He stopped and relished the idea. No one would believe him for sure. He walked home without fear, without stopping.

Next day, Yellow Cloud went to church, with his wife to whom he had disclosed the events of the night. They arrived earlier than usual to listen to the gossip that was sure to circulate—that two suspected practitioners of the arcane art of Maeko-bimossae had sustained fatal injuries or had been killed during the night. Though they discreetly inquired, they learned nothing.

During the services the missionary delivered a blistering sermon on drinking and alcohol. He spoke in Ojibway.

"I am sorry that I must bring up the subject of drinking," he began. "But certain events during the night have prompted me to speak about the evils of drinking. It seems that some people will never learn or having learned refuse to take heed. As long as there is drinking, I will speak about it. It is my duty."

"Yesterday, I went to Blunder Bay to buy a new car so that I could serve you better and carry the Lord's word more widely and more quickly. Last night as I was driving home, one of you, and I will not name any names, the person responsible will know, one of the members of this congregation who was drunk, and whom I was going to pick up, smashed the headlights of my new car.

"I will not say anything about the damage to the car. I will not press any charges, if that person pays for the damages."

The members of the congregation looked around; some sniggered. The preacher looked directly at Yellow Cloud who squirmed. Yellow Cloud's wife giggled. The preacher thundered on.

After services, the Moose Meaters gathered around outside the church to inquire and to guess who had clubbed the preacher's car headlights. Yellow Cloud slunk away.

Don't Make Fun of Old Beliefs

A cold October wind whistled around the corners of the cabin. Inside old Sweetgrass had just finished telling the boys a series of stories of long ago: of Pauguk, the Flying Skeleton; of Cheebiabos, the spirit of Nanabush's brother, who had drowned under mysterious circumstances; and many other grizzly and terrifying tales.

Sweetgrass interrupted the flow of his narrative to light the kerosene lamp and put more wood on the fire, as the night advanced. The corners of the one-room cabin wavered and danced with oddly shaped shadows. An errant limb tapped fitfully at one of the windows.

The boys, six of them, the eldest no more than sixteen, sat silent, enthralled and enchanted, listening to the tales of death, return to life, apparitions, and other phenomena. Although the stories frightened them, their curiosity and desire to appear courageous induced them to request more and more tales from the repertoire of the old story-teller. And he, delighted with his audience, complied with their wishes.

"Tell us about Maeko-bimossae," Clear Water requested.

Every Ojibway child has heard vague rumours about this frightening creature, the "Bear-walker," a being capable of metamorphosis into a horrible variety of shapes. His "medicine" accompanied him in a floating ball of fire, so they said. All the boys murmured their interest.

"I don't think we should talk about Maeko-bimossae," old Sweetgrass replied. "It's not good."

"I don't believe in all that dumb old superstition anyhow," said Fish-Eggs, sniggering his scorn.

"Don't you make fun of the old beliefs," Sweetgrass warned apprehensively.

"What could happen?" Fish-Eggs demanded to know.

"I don't know, but something might. You don't have to believe, as long as you don't make fun of the old ways," Sweetgrass admonished with a shake of his head.

"Well it's a lot of bunk that Maeko-bimossae," Fish-Eggs declared lending emphasis to his disbelief. As if challenging the ancient gods for positive manifestation he added, "I dare any Maeko-bimossae to scare ME. They don't exist. And even if they did I'd kick their tails in."

Sweetgrass drew in a horrified breath between his teeth. "You're just like the rest of the young people, no respect for tradition, no care for the old beliefs that were good enough for your grandfathers. Just you wait. Something's going to happen to you."

"Pooh, pooh." Fish-Eggs blew out two breaths in unconcern. He got his coat, and prepared to depart.

Clear Water came to Sweetgrass' defence in a manner calculated to annoy Fish-Eggs as much as possible. He spoke to the other boys out of the corner of his mouth, in a stage whisper, meant to be overheard.

"Fish-Eggs is all talk. He ain't done nothin' yet, and see how brave he is."

Fish-Eggs whirled around.

"I heard that. You're the one who's scared, not me. You're even scared to go home now. I'm not. And that's where I'm going. Home. Alone. In the dark."

He buttoned his coat. "You guys are goin' to have to go home without me."

Clear Water persisted.

"Hah! You'd lose your pants if you ever saw Maeko-bimossae!"

Fish-Eggs glowered at Clear Water a moment, before he walked over, seized him by the shirt collar, and jerked him up with one hand.

"Listen punk!" he said, "I'd meet anyone, anything, anyplace, anytime."

Clear Water adjusted his shirt with a smirk. He tucked in his shirt-tails once more. "Bet you wouldn' go into that haunted house alone tonight," he challenged.

"That's no test of courage. Why not something harder."Fish-Eggs snapped.

"You're scared. Just making excuses," Clear Water said.

Sweetgrass intervened. "You'd better not go in there. Leave that place alone."

"Why? What's so special about it?" Fish-Eggs asked contemptuously.

Sweetgrass was momentarily confused by the question asked in sarcasm. At last, considering the question a genuine request for knowledge, he began to explain.

"Well, nobody's been able to live there for long. Some of 'em has died; but most of 'em has just got sick. Sometimes people has seen a light bouncing around there at night; sometimes people hear things there even in the daytime. And there's a peculiar smell in that house. Don't seem so bad at first . . . but later. . . . That house is haunted. I think it's cursed. You better not go up there."

"Nuts!" Fish-Eggs snorted. "And I'll prove it. Tonight."

"Just hold on there a minute," Clear Water interrupted. "We gotta have some sorta proof you really went into the house, 'cause I'm not going in with you, and I bet the other guys won't either."

General murmurs of assent were solicited by his questioning look.

"You gotta go in there alone," he continued. "I got it. Take a hammer and a nail, and pound the nail through the top of the big table I seen when I peeked in the kitchen window once. Hey, Sweetgrass! You got a hammer and nails?"

"Yeah, just outside on the porch. The hammer's on the floor and the nails is in a pail," said Sweetgrass reluctantly.

Clear Water opened the door the smallest possible amount, and squirmed through the opening. The sliver of light afforded by the partly opened door allowed him to locate the tools easily, and allowed for minimum heat loss. He reappeared moments later, a hammer in one hand, and a couple of six-inch spikes in the other. Silently he handed the tools to Fish-Eggs.

"Cheez, couldn't you get bigger ones?" Fish-Eggs commented wryly. "Come on! What are you waiting for?"

The other boys put on their coats reluctantly but quickly. They followed Fish-Eggs up the road in the direction of the house they had discussed. It stood on the side of the hill, half a mile away, set back a couple of hundred yards from the road. The subsiding wind blew an eerie song through the bare branches of the gnarled apple trees surrounding the house. Within minutes the boys were standing on the road opposite the gateway leading up to the decrepit old house. They were vastly relieved to see that no bobbing lights had put in an appearance that night. In the late October mist the house was all but invisible, even though the moon glistened through a curtain of haze. Only a denser black shadow parted the wisps of thickening fog.

"You guys can stay here. I won't be long," Fish-Eggs said nonchalantly. "Don't run away. I won't blame you if you do though. Isn't everybody who can be brave."

The boys said nothing. Fish-Eggs was right. He was afraid of nothing, of no one. Their admiration grew as they watched him disappear into the grass that even at this time of year grew tall and rank at the front of the house.

"I wish I was as brave as that." said Cedar Twig in wonder.

"Shshshshsh!!!" Clear Water hissed.

But they heard only the wind rustling the dried leaves on the ground. An owl hooted somewhere in the orchard; the silence was profound.

Bang! Bang! Bang! The sound of hammering emanated from the house, resounded through the trees, was picked up and bounced back from the rock face behind the house, so that it reached the boys with a faint double echo. They shuddered, dug their hands more deeply into their pockets, and their necks more firmly into their collars.

"That Fish-Eggs ain't scared of nothin'," Clear Water whispered in awe. Until this moment he had not believed that Fish-Eggs would actually complete the mission.

The sounds grew louder, ceased. The boys waited in expectation. And waited. And waited. There was a tremendous crash.

"Eeeeeeh!!!! Aaaaaaahh!!!"

The scream was loud and unexpected. There followed a greater crash than they had heard before. Galloping footsteps, fleet and urgent pounded nearby.

The boys' hair rose, their hearts slammed against their ribcages, seemed to leap into their throats to choke them. Without a word and as one, they turned and fled in terror down the road, back to Sweetgrass' cabin. Something pursued them emitting mewling noises.

They burst into the old man's log house. Panting and gasping they looked at one another wildly, unable to speak . . . Fish-Eggs' arm knocked the door back against the wall. He grasped the sides of the doorway and levered himself violently into their midst. Eyes rolling, face ashen, lips quivering, he collapsed upon the floor at their feet. His windbreaker was torn, the left side almost completely gone, as if it had be rent apart by some mighty force. Fish-Eggs lay there, senseless, breathing in uncontrolled and spasmodic gasps.

Sweetgrass bade the boys sit down.

"I told you," he said calmly and with pity.

The old man went to an ancient trunk that was ensconced in the corner. After rummaging briefly he extracted a sock in an acute stage of disrepair.

Opening the circular lid on the top of the box stove, Sweetgrass placed a wire mesh over the aperture. Ritualistically he placed the sock on top of this. As the fire singed the grey wool fibres to brown, he hastily picked up the poker, and expertly turned the sock.

The boys watched with open mouths, speechless. Clear Water knelt beside Fish-Eggs, and tried to roll his windbreaker into a pillow for the head of the unconscious boy. He was so astonished by the ceremony that he was unable to complete the act.

Sweetgrass watched the sock with narrowed eyes. When it began to smoulder and emit thin curling wisps of acrid, blue smoke, he snatched it from the fire.

"Sit him up," he commanded.

Clear Water and Cedar Twig lifted Fish-Eggs into a sitting position, and held him, his head sagging forward limply, chin resting on his chest.

Sweetgrass knelt down and passed the smoking sock beneath Fish-Eggs' nose.

Fish-Eggs gasped, drew in a deep breath, and exploded in a gargantuan sneeze. His head jerked up; he tossed it from side to side to escape the penetrating odour of burning wool. As he did so, he inhaled immensely, and began to cough in short intermittent hacks. The other boys began to cough too, as the smoke assaulted their nostrils.

Fish-Eggs opened his eyes, red and swollen and tearing from the penetrating aroma.

"Be O.K. now," said Sweetgrass nodding his head in satisfaction.

All the boys began to babble at once.

"What happened?"

"What did you see?"

"Cheez, you're brave!"

Fish-Eggs wheezed. He shivered. Unable to blot out the details of his terrifying experience, he endeavoured to recall the exact sequence.

"Got in there. Pounded in the nail. Somebody grabbed me." He stopped, mouth working. "Something got hold of my c-c-c-my coat," he stammered. "Don't . . . after . . . pounded in the . . . coat . . . I . . . don't . . . want . . . to . . . talk . . . about . . . it."

Clear Water and Cedar Twig patted Fish-Eggs' shoulder.

"Cheez you're brave. We shouldn'ta got you to do it."

"Leave 'im be," Sweetgrass suggested. "You can stay all night if you want to sleep on the floor."

No second invitation was needed. The boys settled down close to the fire for a night on the planks, while Sweetgrass went to his bed.

Next morning Sweetgrass was up early, as was his custom. He fried scone (bannock) for the boys, which they smeared generously with lard, and made them innumerable cups of well-sweetened tea.

Breakfast and the morning light raised the spirits of the boys, and they began to discuss a return to the old house, so that they might establish exactly what took place.

Fish-Eggs was quiet and unco-operative.

"I'm not going," he declared tersely. "I'm going home."

With that, he put on his tattered coat and went out the door.

The others were undaunted. They too snatched up their coats, but began their trek up the hill. Even in broad daylight they were apprehensive. Near the house they halted.

For a while no one spoke.

"Whose gonna go in?" one inquired.

"I will," said Clear Water, his voice a little shaky. "I started the whole thing. You guys can come and stand outside the door."

"O.K." all agreed.

They moved forward again stopping on the verandah with its creaking, springy boards.

"Wait here," commanded Clear Water. The door squeaked ominously in the wind, as Clear Water went inside.

The boys shuffled their feet in the silence, and looked at the cobwebs above their heads.

"Haw! Haw! Haw! Haw!" Clear Water guffawed.

He appeared at the door, holding his middle and gasping with laughter. He tried to speak, but again he was overcome.

The boys looked at one another, and back at Clear Water who continued to laugh. Was this hysteria?

Eventually Clear Water gasped, wiped his eyes and mo-

tioned to his friends. "Come on in you guys. Come on and look."
The effort was too much. He began to laugh again, held his
sides, and pointed into the interior.

The boys entered the building, followed by Clear Water
who had managed to control his mirth though with difficulty.

The great table in the kitchen was now laying on its side.
In the centre of the oak planks that made up its top, secured by
a six inch nail, was the missing portion of Fish-Eggs' coat.

For a moment the boys stared at it stupidly. Then the full
implication of the sight hit them.

Cedar Twig began to snigger. The others joined in.

"Haw! Haw! Haw!"

They laughed, looked again, and laughed some more. At
length they managed to stagger out of the door and start home,
giggling occasionally as they remembered.

"Ain't Fish-Eggs brave though," asked Clear Water, expecting no answer. "Ain't he brave?"

What is Sin?

"You must adopt white man's ways; you must become civilized; you must become Christian. Better off that way." The agent said it; the teachers taught it; the preacher preached the message. The Moose Meaters listened, thought about the matter and readily made the instructions part of their daily lives. It made a lot of sense.

For what progress could there be, if Indians in general, and Moose Meaters in particular, were still to hunt with bow and arrow, live in teepees, wear buckskin, and eat wild animals and berries. "Can't live in the past," they said. Did not rifles make hunting easier? Did not houses provide more comfort? Did not cloth enhance appearance? Did not tinned goods provide healthier nourishment? Cheerfully, the Moose Meaters, as progressive-minded as any peoples, learned to speak English, espoused several varieties of Christianity, and married white men and women. Who could do better than that?

But for all their efforts there was precious little help or guidance for the Moose Meat Indians. It seemed that on the one hand they were invited to become Westernized; on the other hand, every impediment was placed in the way either to prevent or retard their rapid acculturation. The clergy condemned among some behaviour like drinking, card playing, dancing of any kind as sinful and meriting eternal damnation. Policemen acting under special laws inscribed in the Indian Act arrested Moose Meaters for transgressing the provisions of the Bible and the Indian Act and consigned them to temporal damnation in jails. What the clergy said was true; the wicked are often punished temporally and eternally. God, it was confusing. Amusements deemed lawful were sinful; certain acts manifestly sinful were lawful.

When and where the white people could drink and be merry, the Moose Meaters could not; when and where the white people could play cards and gamble, the Moose Meaters could not without committing sin; when and where white people could dance, the Moose Meaters could not without pain of sin. How difficult it was to try to be white. How hard to become acculturated.

For some inexplicable reason, circumstances for the Moose Meaters and other Indians did not improve. Even though a large number ceased speaking Ojibway for the sake of English they were not invited to white homes; despite forsaking their own religious practices and beliefs and embracing several shades of Christianity, the Moose Meaters and their kind were still heathen; and although they married whites, their sons and daughters were never white enough to find acceptance in white society. It was rather discouraging. How difficult to remain Ojibway Indian.

But no matter the gravity of the offences in moral or legal terms, the Moose Meaters, having been induced to advantages and promises of acculturation, practised those delights that were considered illegal and venial; surreptitiously, circumspectly, and stealthily perhaps, but practise and enjoy them they did. Damn the consequences.

Of the customs imported from Europe, none was more cherished by the Moose Meaters than the "square dance," an activity that was sanctioned by the Indian Act as quite licit and harmless. However, it was condemned by Canon Law as immoral and as an immediate and remote occasion for sin. The Moose Meaters liked to live dangerously. To the various refined and prescribed movements constituting the "square dance," the enterprising people of Moose Meat Point added jumping, pirouettes, leap-frog, stamping, clucking, hooting, whistling, yelling and a hundred other little refinements from their war scalping dances long in disuse but not forgotten. Anthropologists and behavioural scientists alike would have been enthralled by the ingenious admixture of two disparate cultures.

So much did the Moose Meaters enjoy "square dancing" that they met at least once a week in some private home to polish their techniques and to exercise.

There was always an occasion for celebration; the successful and safe return of some native son or daughter from an expedition to the white man's cities; a bountiful catch of fish or game; the receipt of four dollars of annuity money from the government's largesse; a birth, a baptism, a wedding and sometimes the demise of someone who had lived too long and needed a rousing send-off. Often the celebration did not need a reason. Ojibway have always been willing and excellent celebrants.

Had there been a dance hall and had the church permitted dancing, the Moose Meaters might not have resorted to clandestine meetings. As it was, there was no public dance hall. Besides that, the Moose Meaters had blended an immoral act, dancing, with an illegal act, drinking.

After a decision to hold a party was made, all that was needed was a fiddler, a caller, one or two buckets of home-made wine manufactured from bran, yeast cake, sugar, raisins and three days of fierce, bubbling fermentation. These were the basic components for a good house party.

One Saturday night, while the dancers whirled like dervishes, leaped and whooped as if performing a good old-fashioned scalp dance to "swing your partners in your corners all," the door flew open without a knock, and through it stepped the priest, a dark scowl shrouding his face.

He did not have to say anything to command silence. The fiddler whose arms had been flailing ground to a slow halt; the dancers who had been stamping their feet and howling through "dip and dive" halted and slunk away from the centre of the floor; the caller coughed.

Zawanimkee (Yellow Thunder), owner of the house and host to the party paled visibly. He secretly set aside his mug before he stepped forward to greet the priest.

"Come in, Fauder," he said to the priest who was already well inside and standing in the middle of the floor glowering at all those present.

The priest did not acknowledge the invitation nor the welcome. Eyes ablaze like coals, nostrils distended like gills, he bellowed.

"SINNERS! YOU SINNERS! DANCING! DRINKING! Dancing on the night before Sunday. Drinking on the eve of the Sabbath." He was horrified and scandalized. "You are sinning. All of you. You are breaking the law, everyone of you. And some of you were to confession tonight. And none of you will go to church tomorrow." The priest paused.

The dancers stood still. Some of them were slightly unsteady on their feet owing to the twirls of "swing your partners" reinforced by the pot of the home-made brew; but they stood still.

"How'd we sins, Fauder?" one of the dancers, Kagige (Forever) by name, dared to ask. He was puzzled.

The priest whirled around and aimed a quaking righteous finger in front of the nose of the impertinent and startled Kagige.

"You!" The priest said, "You are the worst. You know the sin. You pretend not to know it. And pretending not to know the sin makes you doubly guilty. You have sinned. And you try to make a fool of me. You know better than that. You went to school, a Catholic school. You should be a good example to the others. Instead you are the worst example of what a good Catholic should be." The words rattled out of the priest's mouth.

"I don' know what you mean, Fauder," stammered the shaken and bewildered Kagige. "We didn' do no sin yet." Kagige was certain.

"Ah, hah", the priest snarled, "that's just it. You haven t committed any sin yet. That's what you think. You have already committed at least two. You have been drinking; that's a sin. You have been dancing; that's a sin. That makes it two. By being present at an occasion that is likely to lead to sin, you are sinning. That makes it three. You know that you must never place yourself in a situation that will lead your soul to everlasting damnation in the flames of hell. And if you find yourself in such a situation you must remove yourself from the occasion of temptation. No telling how many other sins you may have already committed. No telling how many more you would have committed tonight, if I had not come."

The words burst out in a torrent, a frothy flood of theology that bewildered the celebrants. While Father Beauchamp was expostulating upon morality, his keen eyes sharp in the discovery of sin, bespied a battered dipper nestling brazenly and openly in the middle of the table where it ought not to have been. Sniffing loudly, Father strode over, seized the offending dipper by the handle. Some home brew splashed out, soiling the good Father's sleeve and drenching his hand.

Father whirled around once more to face Kagige, and like a prosecutor closing in upon a perjurer, snarled:

"I thought you said there was no sinning. You lied. You knew there was wine here. You knew there was drinking. You, yourself, have been drinking. Your breath reeks. Your eyes are bleary. Your speech is slurred. Your hands shake. And drinking is a sin. You have the audacity, the effrontery to tell me that there was no sinning."

Kagige could only squirm and blanch under the barrage.

Turning to the others, the priest hissed, "Go home! Now! Right now! Make sure that you go to confession and church tomorrow."

At his command, Kagige and the other revellers began sullenly but quietly to put on their hats and coats. A couple managed to go out the door. But Father was not finished with them.

"You!" he barked at Pitawaniquot (Between the Clouds). "If it weren't for you and that accursed instrument of sin, these people would not be committing sin tonight or any other night. Because of you, many sins have been committed not only on this evening but many evenings past. Don't you realize that you are the immediate occasion for the sins that have been committed or might have been committed here tonight? Don't you realize that if you were not present, there would be no party and no sin?" The flood of words continued unabated.

Pitawaniquot was stunned. He almost dropped his beloved fiddle as he put it back affectionately in the case. The thought that he, a fiddler, could inspire and incite sin terrified him. He prayed a little. He tried to think. In all the years of playing "Golden Slippers" or "The Virginia Reel," he could not remember arousing in himself or harbouring lecherous or impure thoughts during or after the renditions. His sole purpose had been to add to the enjoyment of the dancing and parties. Still the possibility unnerved him.

Along with the dancers and under the watchful eye of the priest, Pitawaniquot left the premises and vanished into the night.

Zawanimkee and his wife had to face the priest alone and listen to a stern lecture on the evils of drink. They, like Pitawaniquot, were responsible for any and all sins that had been and would have been committed that night. God, to whom they were answerable, would punish them in the next world. The police and the judge would, were he to inform the authorities, throw the book at Zawanimkee and his wife before throwing them in jail. Zawanimkee and his wife realizing the enormity of their offence, contritely promised to go to confession and to discontinue hosting parties.

Sunday morning's congregation listened to a blistering sermon on the evils of dancing. Many wondered who and what had incited Father's wrath; those who were privy to the secret, smiled.

But no sermon, not even the threat of eternal damnation and temporal punishment, deterred the square dancers or the wine makers. The only thing that threatened to put an end to the happy affair was the imminent refusal of Pitawaniquot to continue to play. Frankly he was intimidated not only by the thought of hell-fires but also because he was responsible for numerous other sins in addition to those of dancing and drinking. But he was essential; he was indispensable. Without him, without music, there could be no dancing. He could not quit, he had to be persuaded to continue.

Kagige, who was educated and had some knowledge of theology was delegated to persuade Pitawaniquot to continue playing. It was hard trying to convince the only fiddler on the Moose Meat Point Indian Reserve to keep on playing. It was not enough to tell Pitawaniquot that he was crucial and was needed. Kagige had to resort to moral argument. He assured his friend on good authority that were they to be found guilty on judgement day and dispatched to hell, he would accept all blame and responsibility for the sins, and even all the sins that might be committed by any of the dancers whatever the occasion. Kagige told the fiddler that he would plead on Pitawaniquot's behalf for exoneration.

Pitawaniquot may not have exactly believed that his guilt could be transferred to another, but he was moved by this selfless act on the part of his friend. He was glad. The Ojibway may have forgotten many of their traditions but assuming responsibility for others and taking blame were not among them. Assured that he would not be implicated in the here-present or in the here-after, Pitawaniquot resumed playing, but just to make sure, he culled "The Devil's Dream" and "Oh, Susannah" from his repertoire as tunes most likely to provoke erotic and lecherous passions.

The dancers continued to meet secretly. To evade priest and police, the place of the dances was rotated furtively from week to week and from house to house. But the priest was not less cunning nor less resourceful than were the Indian square dancers. Uncannily he appeared at every dance, always at the moment when the apex of gaiety had been reached, and always at the time when the home-brew was only partly consumed.

Saturday after Saturday the dancers, the wine makers, the fiddler, and the caller congregated only to be dispersed. None was discouraged, not even the priest who hinted darkly and ominously that the police would have to be called and perhaps even excommunication would have to be invoked. The Moose Meaters began to hold their dances farther and further from the main village.

Finally the square dance loving Indians scheduled one of their Saturday night November dances in a remote part of the reserve some nine or ten miles from the main village. To forestall any interference in their party by the clergy, the celebrants held a war council to discuss and decide upon the most suitable way of dealing with the priest. Kagige was for assaulting the priest and even raising a small party of men to howl and shout outside the priest's residence for several hours every night for several nights. The others dissuaded him from undertaking such a foolish and wasteful course. Pitawaniquot suggested posting a watch at the gate in full military style to report on the arrival of any outsiders. The men would take turns at sentry duty, changing shift every half hour. At the approach of someone the sentry was to run to the house and give the alarm. The patrons would then abandon the house seeking shelter in the nearby woods.

"I was thinking," Pitawaniquot said after agreement had been reached on the tactics to be followed, "I don't think we should do anything to the priest. Never know what he might do. I been thinking. It's not the priest's fault entirely. It's that horse. It's the fault of that horse."

Kagige startled, broke in, "How'd you figure that? You can't blame the horse. It's that priest, and nobody else."

"Well," Pitawaniquot continued, looking down at his rubber boots, "it's like this. If it weren't for me, you people wouldn't sin. If it weren't for this fiddle, I wouldn't lead you people to sin. If it weren't for that horse, the priest would not get anywhere. Same thing."

Kagige got up and shook Pitawaniquot's hand. "You know, I never thought of that. It makes a lot of horse sense. We should punish that horse. He's to blame." Everyone agreed by nodding.

The weather that November eve was ill—sleet and wind—unfit for the ministry, but fitting for corporal pleasures.

That night during the fifth shift, Water-Hole, leaning against the gate post near the road, heard the sound of an approaching horse and buggy, splashing in the mud. He ran to the house, shouted, "Someone's coming" and dashed back to the gate hiding behind a clump of bushes. From this vantage point, he observed the priest pull up, and tie his panting horse to the gate post.

The priest strode to the darkened quiet house. Water-Hole went into action. He broke off a sapling. Going to the horse who shied at his approach, Water-Hole first soothed the horse. Then he unhitched the animal from the buggy and untied him from the gate post.

"What's going on there?" the priest yelled in the darkness down the roadway.

"Hah!", Water-Hole, spat out, "if it hadn't been for you, you damned horse, the priest wouldn't have come. You brought him here," he said addressing the horse.

Then he gave the beast a sharp blow with the sapling; the horse galloped in terror down the road and back to the village.

The priest no longer interfered with the square dancers of the parishioners, the rules were relaxed and the Moose Meaters became even more accomplished in dancing.

Secular Revenge

Kitug-Aunquot (Mottled Cloud) long resisted the blandishments of Episcopalians, Methodists, Anglicans, Catholics, United Church members and a few other brands of denominations to join their congregation and become a Christian. Not that he had anything against any of them, nor that he so cherished his traditional beliefs and ceremonies that he had clung to them and would not have given them up. Rather it was for practical reasons that the old man remained an unconverted heathen. He did not wish, by joining one persuasion, to offend the others, especially his friends who belonged to one or other of the many denominations. Besides that, he could see very little difference between any one of them. He chose to remain neutral.

Eventually old Kitug-Aunquot was persuaded to take instructions not so much by the theology of but more by the Ojibway-speaking abilities of the resident Roman Catholic missionary. The old man had little trouble understanding or accepting the Ten Commandments or the basic tenets of the church. They made a lot of sense. In the fifty-eighth year of his life, Kitug-Aunquot was baptized.

He loved going to church and considering the distance that he had to travel every Sunday, Kitug-Aunquot's efforts to attend mass once a week were laudable. However, it was not long before the old man realized that being Catholic was not as easy as he had at first thought it to be. He was, moreover, disappointed by the changed attitude and mood of the priest. No longer was the priest amiable, conciliatory, and compassionate as he had been; now he was hostile, dictatorial, and dispassionate. Kitug-Aunquot began to regret his decision. Nevertheless he continued to go to church as often as he could.

What bewildered Kitug-Aunquot were the Six Commandments of the church, which had not been explained to him during his instructions prior to his admission into the church. He was as confused as anyone else.

The one church law that most disturbed him was, "Thou shalt fast and abstain on the days appointed." It was easy enough to understand; but it was hard to observe even though the Ojibway were experienced fasters, accustomed to long and serious food shortages at times.

It was the number of obligatory fasting days that annoyed him. As Kitug-Aunquot saw it, the frequency of days requiring fast and abstinence—fifty-two Fridays, forty days more during Lent, to which were added Rogation days—all were designed more to foster perpetual hunger and suffering rather than the growth of grace and piety. One day in three to be spent in self-denial, was too much.

However, he took comfort in the fact that in two years' time, at age sixty, he would, like those under the age of sixteen, be exempted from fasting though he would still have to abstain from eating meat. Secretly he wished he were a fully-fledged farmer, lumberjack, or fisherman so that he would be eligible for immediate exemption and relief.

In the meantime, he had to fast and abstain. Otherwise he would sin and qualify for eternal damnation. Even though he could eat meat if "he had nothing else to eat" on the appointed days, he still had to fast. That little concession meant little to Kitug-Aunquot who too often had little else.

It was as difficult to interpret these theological matters, as it was to enforce them. The local missionary, Father Beauchamp, tried his best, thundering and expounding on them from the pulpit, inflicting heavy penance upon those guilty of sinning against the laws of fast and abstinence. The Indians listened and confessed. They, too, tried their best, never suggesting in their confusion that surely such a law must change from week to week.

What could not be achieved from the pulpit was explained in private visit by the missionary to the houses of the faithful.

No missionary was more zealous or scrupulous to duty and church law than was Father Beauchamp, S.J. Determined that no member of his flock should be damned through ignorance of Church Law or wilful transgression, Father Beauchamp paid frequent personal visits to his constituents.

Not having seen Kitug-Aunquot at church for a couple of weeks, Father Beauchamp, worried and vexed, decided to call on the old man.

It was Friday, and there were no urgent matters to attend to; a good day to go. The morning was cold, and the crisp snow crunched under the Father's snowshoes as he plodded along. The way was long, perhaps some four miles. These Indians, especially the old ones, had a perverse habit of erecting their homes in remote and inaccessible locations. Father puffed his way through bushes, and around trees, the cold making his eyes water.

He arrived at Kitug-Aunquot's log house at noon, relieved to see smoke wafting blissfully from the rusty stovepipe protruded from the roof at a drunken angle. Father, weary of leg, slippéd out of his snowshoes and hung them from a nail on the side of the cabin. He knocked commandingly upon the door.

"Peendigaen (Come in)," responded Kitug-Aunquot in a muffled voice.

Father lifted the latch and pushed the door open, dislodging several blankets placed there to insulate the shack from the cold. The priest squeezed past this impediment and into the interior. Old Kitug-Aunquot, sitting at his table, made no move to get up. Disrespectfully, he continued to munch on his food. Father apologized as he picked up the blankets, restored them to the nails on either side of the door, and smoothed them out.

Satisfied with his handiwork, Father turned to Kitug-Aunquot who chewed contentedly on his meal.

"I've come to see how you were," the priest said cheerfully. He was about to add, " . . . and why you haven't been to church," when a sweeping glance at Kitug-Aunquot's table stopped him.

The priest was horrified; he quaked; he paled. There upon a tin plate modestly nestled half a roll of bologna; another portion was blushingly lodged between two large crusts of bannock, cradled in the fist of Kitug-Aunquot; and there was a strong presumption that another sinful morsel was in the old man's mouth. What was worse, Kitug-Aunquot was devouring the bologna with relish, without remorse. The priest was appalled. It was Friday, and there was ample evidence that Kitug-Aunquot had other food in his cabin. A pile of potatoes gently steamed on a platter in the middle of the table.

Father Beauchamp seethed with rage as Kitug-Aunquot took another sensual bite without looking up. Father collected his wrath.

"Kitug-Aunquot," the priest managed in a loud, quivering tone, "Don't you know that you are committing a MORTAL SIN? Don't you know that if you were to DIE NOW, you would go STRAIGHT TO HELL and BURN FOREVER? Bologna on FRIDAY!"

"I got nutting else Fauder," said Kitug-Aunquot unimpressed.

He swallowed with evident satisfaction.

"What do you mean you've got nothing else," demanded the priest. "You've got lots of potatoes. Why don't you eat fish?"

Kitug-Aunquot took another unpenitent bite.

"Ice too tick. Can't catch no fish," retorted the old man through his mouthful of bologna.

Father was dismayed. Not only was Kitug-Aunquot unrepentant, he was defiant. He had enough gall to argue with a priest.

It was obvious that neither threats nor reason were going to detach Kitug-Aunquot from the lustful enjoyment of his bologna. The priest decided that he would have to resort to his authority. Often it was the only method that could persuade some recalcitrant Indian.

"Put away that meat," resounded Father.

"Ain't meat," the old man shot back.

Father Beauchamp was stunned.

"What do you mean 'it ain't meat!' It is meat! It is made of meat, many different kinds of meat. The church says it's meat. The stores call it meat. Everyone knows that it's meat. Only YOU try to deny it. Meat! You wouldn't admit the difference between meat and porridge if it didn't suit you. You are a wicked, sinful old man. You know the laws of the church. Still you persist in breaking them. Someday you will burn in hell forever. God have mercy on your poor soul."

Kitug-Aunquot picked up all the bologna and heaved it into the corner. He sat staring at the floor.

Father Beauchamp, still fuming, walked out.

On Monday, Mishibinishima (Big Shield), a friend, came for a visit. He told Kitug-Aunquot that the following day, Shrove Tuesday, the church was conducting a wood-cutting bee. All the men with axes and saws were asked to cut wood; all those with horses and sleighs were to haul the wood to the church. Would Kitug-Aunquot, who owned a team of horses, haul wood for the church?

"No," said Kitug-Aunquot.

Mishibinishima was surprised, but not easily discouraged.

"Afterward dere's a big feas' for everyone at de hall at 6.00. Den der's a dance. Pretty soon its Lent. Can't eat much den.Can't dance much den, too," he added thoughtfully.

Kitug-Aunquot considered the food and the dance; he decided to make an effort. Finally he agreed: "Okay."

Very early the next day, Kitug-Aunquot harnessed the horses and hitched them to the sleigh. He set out to haul the wood from the bush where it would be cut. On the way he passed a saw mill. He stopped, pondered, turned his team around, and headed for home.

At the barn, Kitug-Aunquot removed the four corner stakes from his sleigh and installed a box. He picked up a pickaxe and a shovel, threw them on the sleigh and then proceeded down to the mill. Working furiously first with pick and then with shovel Kitug-Aunquot loaded his sleigh in no time at all. It was easier than going into the bush for a load; and faster too.

His sleigh loaded, the old man drove his team to the church where he deposited his cargo.

"What's that?" a friend asked.

"Sawdust" Kitug-Aunquot replied smirking. The friend looked on, quizzically.

All day Kitug-Aunquot laboured, hauling load after load, drawing stares, smiles and laughter from the other teamsters. The pile of sawdust at the back of the church grew larger.

It was getting dark, when Kitug-Aunquot delivered his last load. The other teamsters were also finished. The horses tired. As Kitug-Aunquot was unloading his final cargo, Father Beauchamp, face flushed, cheeks puffing out like those of a tuba player came ploughing through the deep snow.

"Kitug-Aunquot,what in the name of damnation are you doing?" asked the priest.

"Bring' wood, fauder," Kitug-Aunquot answered calmly.

"But this is sawdust. It isn't wood. Kitug-Aunquot! Are you trying to make a fool of me?" the priest demanded, his hands on his hips.

"Fauder, you say boloney, meat. Okay; den, sawdus' is woods," Kitug-Aunquot declared with a twinkle in his eye.

The other Moose Meaters sniggered.

The Root of Evil

The day for the Moose Meat Point Indian Reserve bazaar began auspiciously; the sun shining splendidly in a cloudless sky; the mass attended by everyone in the village. Father was pleased, said an extra prayer of thanksgiving.

Then the festivities commenced, albeit slowly. The Indians cautiously inspected the various articles for sale; the children examined the games of chance; a few began to practise for the ball game. Father Marshall, S.J., like a general gathering his army, was busy issuing a barrage of instructions to the clucking members of the Ladies' Auxiliary.

By mid-morning the mood of the bazaar was changing either for the better or the worse, depending on the point of view. For some of the men, events were fast improving; for the Reverend Marshall, S.J. matters were deteriorating. His bazaar was taking on the aspect of a Bacchanalian revel.

Father, exasperated and alarmed, was decisive.

"Come here," he summoned two young boys who were wandering aimlessly by. "Go find out where the men are drinking and come back and tell me." So saying, the priest handed each of the boys a sparkling quarter.

"Okay, Fauder," the boys gleefully replied, dashing off immediately in the general direction of the concession stands, looking from right to left all the while.

When they had reached the booths without discovering the source of the problem that was causing Father's dilemma, the boys shrugged philosophically, and applied themselves to the games with vigour and delight. They had, after all, watched carefully for the fifty-yard distance they had covered. With fervour, they had observed both sides of the path. Now they could stop and enjoy the fruits of their zeal.

Father surveyed the grounds and the congregation trying to detect a suspicious bulge in someone's pocket or to observe a surreptitious movement. He would, he was determined, catch them. No bootlegger was going to ruin his bazaar, or outwit him. He was certain that the booze had been smuggled in by some enterprising but illicit vendor from nearby Blunder Bay.

Already the star pitcher, the short-stop, and the catcher were showing tipsy good humour from banging back a few too many. One or two more swigs of the fruit of the vine and none of them would be able to find the bases so the baseball game scheduled for 1.00 P.M. would either have to be cancelled, or given up by default to the Blunder Bay team. Something had to be done fast, while there was still time.

Several ladies, broad of beam, aft and fore, accosted Father timidly.

"Fauder, we sol' all dem old clothes awready. Can you git somemore?"

With smiles, they handed the priest $4.00, the proceeds representing the profits realized from the sale of the clothes. The women giggled in Ojibway, and Father's frown changed into a benign smile.

"Of course," the priest replied cheerfully, his spirit uplifted as he turned to go toward the rectory. At the same time his mind wandered in the vista'd world of finance and profits. The revenue-making powers of old clothes never ceased to amaze him. His church would certainly get a new paint job.

"Goo' mowmin', Fauder," came a loud and joyful greeting.

Father instantly returned to the world of reality, represented in the flushed face of Front Feather. His smile faded into a glower as he was confronted with the happy visage of the Indian.

At that moment Father would have relished seizing Front Feather by the throat and shaking the concupiscence out of him. Manfully, Father resisted the urge. First of all at 6'3" and 230 pounds, Front Feather was too big; Father, himself, was scarcely 5'6". But Father desisted for another reason. This was the first time Front Feather had deigned to speak to him or to come this close to the church establishment. As long as there was a chance of bringing Front Feather into the fold from the realm of the lost, it was, the priest felt, better to cultivate Front Feather's amiability than to alienate him.

With as much friendliness and composure as he was capable of mustering, Father returned the salutation.

"Good morning, Front Feather. Good to see you here."

"Fauder, I ain't been to church for long times, me. But one dese days I goin' come," declared Front Feather, before Father could say anything more.

Father was thankful that Front Feather had taken the burden of conversation from him; he had always had difficulty speaking cheerfully to inebriates. Not wishing to prolong the talk and anxious to deliver a new supply of old clothes to the tables, he still felt that he had to respond to Front Feather's declaration of intent to come to church.

"Good. I'll be looking for you," was the best Father could do.

He detached himself from Front Feather, who continued to grin at him with unabashed delight. Father, followed by the corpulent members of the Ladies' Auxiliary, who continued to discuss the quality of the old clothes, made off toward the rectory.

Father was not listening to the ladies; he was decidedly uneasy. He could not forget Front Feather, and his conscience began to bother him. Putting off Front Feather, Father reasoned, could mean damnation for both of them: damnation for Front Feather for non-attendance of church, for intoxication, for lechery, for swearing and for other sins at which Father could guess shrewdly; his was an active but practical imagination. It could mean damnation for Father, himself, passing up the opportunity to save Front Feather's soul. That Front Feather's contrition, and new found interest in religion were in all probability generated by Four Aces or Slinger's, particularly insidious types of cheap wine, did not make matters easier. Providence operated in mysterious ways. It could even work through wine. For this reason the plea could not be ignored with impunity.

Father, slightly depressed, sighed with consternation. The day was worsening. Why could the drunks not have waited for another occasion? Why at his bazaar?

Determined to return to Front Feather later, Father hurried on toward the rectory. One of the women tagging along behind, left off her chatter suddenly and stopped, open-mouthed. What she saw was so bizarre, and so unique that she felt she must tell the priest immediately. She hurried after him, touched his arm shyly, but with determination, and reported the phenomenon in tones of awe.

"Fauder, de men is going to church,"

Father, startled by this intelligence, felt his day improving. He looked in the direction of her outflung finger.

It was true. Father's heart glowed at what he beheld. The word "miracle" came to his mind instantly. He stopped to observe more closely.

There at the bottom of the church steps were three brown parishioners. Two more were perched on the railing of the landing. Father's heart swelled; the Lord worked in mysterious ways. Momentarily, Father forgot Front Feather. Father's heart expanded more.

Then it constricted; something was wrong. Father's eyes narrowed as he watched three parishioners emerge from the church with some difficulty, laughing loudly and gesticulating wildly. Such conduct was hardly the manner of piety and reverance. It was more the deportment of the frivolous and the impious.

Father shaded his narrowed eyes with a steady hand. As the three carefree visitors to the chapel descended the steps, those who had been waiting on the landing entered. Those occupying the steps moved up to the landing, and, three more parishioners, as if by signal, moved from the crowd to take up a position on the stairway.

Father squinted; his heart squeezed. It was almost like, too much like, Forty Hours Devotion. The Indian adorers were going into the church in relays. This bore investigation. It was both puzzling and pleasing.

But first the old clothes. Father conducted his entourage of corpulent ladies to the rectory, distributed a new consignment of old clothes, and ushered them out. Then he turned toward the chapel.

At his approach, the Indians waiting on the stairway and its landing slunk away quickly and vanished into the crowd before he could question them. Father wondered at this strange behaviour. Why would adorers withdraw?

Father Marshall walked briskly up the steps. He opened the door to the vestibule and was almost knocked to the floor by two blithe parishioners who came barging out of the church basement door. Father gasped to recapture his breath. The Indians tried unsuccessfully to suppress their gaiety.

"What are you doing in the cellar?" the priest demanded bristling.

The Indians shuddered, looked sheepish.

"D-d-drinking root-beer F-F-Fauder," stammered one of the natives.

Father was dumbfounded and incredulous.

"Liars! Liars!" Father thundered. "Sister Alphonsus sent that root-beer for this afternoon during the ball game. Get out! And stay out!"

The Indians hastily retreated from the church. Father opened the cellar door. Laughter and loud talk assailed his ears; the pungent, sweet odour of root-beer and the sharper smell of wine assaulted his nose. Father was enraged at this open defilement of the church.

"Get out!" he shouted to anyone or anything that might lurk in the dark.

At his command some seven or eight figures stood up swiftly and skulked out as silently as phantoms.

Alone in the dark, dank, and silent cellar, Father peered blindly into the blackness, and groped around for the offending wine. He could find none. Still the odour of the wine remained, tantalizing and strong, but always just out of reach. On the floor sat the root-beer barrel, a darker shadow.

As his eyes became accustomed to the gloom, Father made out the shapes of two tomato cans resting on the root-beer barrel. He lifted one of the tins; some liquid splashed on his hand. He sniffed the can; he surreptitiously tasted the liquid on his hand carefully with the tip of his tongue; nostrils quivering, he smelled the contents of the root-beer barrel. Wine, wine, wine.

Father's anger and indignation evaporated. Piously he forgave the drunken members of his flock. The bazaar was saved. The ball game would go on. There would be no hangovers on the morrow. But there would be no root-beer for refreshment that afternoon.

As he locked the door of the church, he decided thoughtfully that he would have to recommend to Sister Alphonsus of the Daughters of Saint Joseph that she alter her root-beer recipe.

The Power of Prayer

Keeshig (Cedar) and the Judge, with Cawiss (Herring) and
Half-Calf some five or six yards behind, shuffled their way up
Blunder Bay's Main Street now coated with ice deposited by a
recent storm which had lashed the town with freezing rain.
Poles glittered in the halo of light from streetlights. Every wire,
every fire hydrant had its own coating of ice. The side-walks
glistened, treacherously slick and dangerous under foot.

Back and forth between the two groups of men scampered
"Almighty" in a playful mood. At nineteen, she was kittenish
and frolicsome, running forward with a devil-may-care attitude
to hurl herself upon Keeshig and the Judge, bringing her hands
down on their shoulders and causing them to fall in a heap
amidst the laughter of the whole group. Or she would walk between Cawiss and Half-Calf, her arms around their necks, flick
her foot out and trip one of them, whereupon they would fall in
a tangled heap, laughing and squealing in delight. It was fun.

Cawiss had ventured forth that morning to get supplies
and to pick up his sister, Almighty, from her job at the local
hairdresser's, since she was to spend the week-end torturing his
wife's hair into a more acceptable coiffure. Along the road he
had picked up the other men, who had decided to while away a
rainy afternoon in a pool-hall. A sudden drop in temperature,
and a friend who was generous with his liquor had caused the
state of affairs in which they now found themselves. Slightly
inebriated and unsteady as they were, Almighty and the ice
made walking a hazard. To complicate matters even more, Cawiss had misplaced his car, but the little group were hopeful of its
quick recovery. In the meantime, Almighty's high spirits
affected them all.

90

Almighty whispered to Cawiss and Half-Calf, "Watch this!"

She trotted forward spritely, flung herself upon Keeshig and the Judge, sending them flopping and flailing to the icy surface. She, herself, landed on top of the pile.

"Eeeeeyouh!" she screamed.

"Ooooooohhh!" she moaned.

She writhed this way and that holding her shoulder.

"Ahahahahahahahah!" she groaned.

Keeshig and the Judge stopped giggling abruptly, and knelt by the side of the stricken Almighty.

"What's wrong? What happened?" they inquired with hoarse anxiety.

"Ooooooh! Aaaaaaaah!" was all Almighty could manage.

Half-Calf and Cawiss slid to a stop and knelt down beside Almighty and the others.

A few passers-by stopped to look, to determine the cause of the anguished cries. Windows flew open on either side of the street. Doors were flung open. People came out to investigate the source of the rumpus.

"What happened? What's the matter?" they asked, forming an ever broadening circle around the group. Almighty was enjoying the attention. She languished on the sidewalk.

"Ah, it's only a bunch of Indians!" one bystander said with disappointment.

"Yeah. Musta been drinking," observed another with disgust.

Keeshig put his coat underneath Almighty's head. He stroked her brow to comfort her as she continued to moan and toss, observing the reaction she was producing, her eyelashes veiling her eyes.

"It's all right," he said to the crowd. "We'll get a doctor."

"What's going on here?" boomed out the voice of Corporal Don Key, the town policeman, who, with a fellow officer, elbowed aside the crowd to get near to the victim and her companions. "What happened?"

"I seen it all, officer," whined a rotund man in a red plaid mackintosh coat. He shifted in his rubber boots, whose tops he had rolled down to mid-calf, and into which he had thrust the legs of his pants. "I was just across the street there, when these Indians started to fight, and the girl got hurt. Oh, I seen it all."

"Good," said the policeman, assessing the honesty of the witness with steely eyes. "We need all the witnesses we can get."

"Now, what started the fight?" the officer asked the four Indians.

"Wasn't any fight. We weren't fighting," protested Keeshig without getting up. He patted Almighty's head.

"Is the girl hurt?" asked the officer.

"Guess so," Keeshig muttered.

"Bad?"

"Guess so."

"Where?"

"Shoulder, I guess."

The officer knelt down and grasped Almighty's shoulder gently. She stopped moaning at once and regarded him thoughtfully through half-closed lids.

"Where does it hurt?" the policeman asked pressing Almighty's arm from wrist to shoulder. Almighty giggled and then lost her temper.

"Hey, you. Keep you hands to yourself," she shouted indignantly. "You ain't no doctor. What's the matter with you anyhow?" She sat up.

"You're not hurt. Your arm's not broken," the officer fumed. "You're just pretending. Why! you're feigning injury. I can charge you with disorderly conduct, and if you don't stop hitting my arm I can charge you with assaulting an officer."

"If you'da minded you own business nothing woulda happened," Almighty blurted out.

"Listen." The officer outshouted Almighty. "I can charge you with disorderly conduct, disturbing the peace, creating a disturbance, and public mischief. Do you understand? I can arrest you."

Almighty was horrified. Keeshig, Cawiss, Half-Calf, and the Judge immediately slipped away unnoticed, since all attention was focused on Almighty.

She jumped up. Don Key clutched at her. Almighty struggled. On such a street, neither could retain their balance and they fell in a heap, Almighty on the bottom, Officer Don Key on the top.

"Eeeeeeyouh! Aaaaaaaahh!" Almighty cried holding her leg, rocking back and forth weeping.

"Quit pretending," advised the officer brushing himself off.

"Eeeeeeyouh!" Almighty moaned. "You broke my leg." And she cried in earnest.

Corporal Don Key called to his partner, "Get the others. Arrest them for disturbing the peace, and I think they were drinking."

"Yeah!" murmured the crowd.

The partner dashed off.

"Now, you . . . " he said glaring down at Almighty who continued to moan.

"Take me to the hospital," she managed to say. "I need a doctor."

Don Key was thoroughly alarmed, and since Almighty could not stand, he scooped her up, settled her over his shoulder, and strode off in the direction of the hospital. Some of the crowd dispersed, convinced that the action was over; others followed the policeman toward the hospital expressing displeasure with Almighty for having disturbed the tranquillity of Blunder Bay.

The policeman was solicitous. "Keep your leg still," he suggested as he entered the hospital. And indeed Almighty's leg was broken.

Constable Oscar Quiver returned, red and puffing to report that the accomplices had made a clean getaway.

"Never mind," assured Officer Don Key grimly. "I know those guys. We can round them up tomorrow."

Early the next morning, the Corporal and the Constable went to the Moose Meat Point Reserve to apprehend Cawiss, Keeshig, Half-Calf, and the Judge. It took all morning to round them up from various places on the reserve, but the police persevered.

The officers charged the Indians with all the crimes they had outlined on the previous night, and added the charge of drunkenness, on which all the other charges hinged. In truth the four Moose-Meaters had been red of eye, and unsteady of hand, but they were sober, and in view of the circumstances, likely to stay that way. They were taken to jail where they were locked in separate cells to await trial on Monday morning.

On Sunday morning, the turnkey came through the cell area announcing the conducting of church services for those who wished to attend. Mass for Catholics was to be held at 9.00 o'clock in the chapel, to be followed by a service for protestants at 10.00 A.M..

The turnkey walked back by the cells twirling his keys and humming "Bringing in the sheaves" when the Judge was given what can only be regarded as a divine inspiration.

"Psst! Hey Warden!" he called to the turnkey. "Commere."

"Huh? Whaddayah want?" the turnkey asked.

"Can us Indians pray too?" the Judge inquired.

The turnkey raised his eyebrows. "I didn't know Indians prayed."

"Oh yeah. We pray. Like to pray. But we pray in our own language," the Judge insisted.

"Just let me check with the Warden. I'll let you know in a few minutes," and the turnkey disappeared. Shortly afterward he was back.

"Warden says that it's O.K. You guys can pray in the chapel after the others is finished."

"Thank you. Thank you," called the Judge after the departing turnkey.

He lay on his bunk to wait.

Shortly after 11.00 o'clock the turnkey returned to fetch the Moose Meaters and herded them toward the chapel. Inside the Judge went straight to the pulpit; Cawiss, Keeshig, and Half-Calf sat down in the back pew.

Lifting his eyes heavenward, the Judge piously began his sermon in Ojibway.

"Waewaenih bizindimook (Attend carefully to what I have to say)."

The Moose Meaters regarded him owlishly.

"Mee maunda gae inaudjimowing (This is the story that we shall release.)"

Keeshig, Cawiss and Half-Calf looked at the turnkey and the guard at the back of the church apprehensively. The two men were listening with interest.

"Aungwaumzik! Amen, naunigotinong kidook (Take care that you say 'Amen' occasionally.)"

"Amen," the men breathed, enthralled.

The turnkey and the guard at the back clasped their hands and bowed their heads in prayer, hastily echoing the "Amen." It was evident that they were affected by the solemn occasion, and the reverence and piety of the prisoners. It was also evident that they understood not one word of Ojibway.

The Judge continued, "Aubidaek tchi naussaubaudjimowing (We must tell the same story.)"

There was much wisdom in the observation.

"Kaween k'miniquaemissimnaubum shkotae-waubo . . . (We were not drinking liquor . . .)"

"Amen!" responded the men.

On and on the Judge preached with passion and fervour. No minister had ever delivered such a moving, heart-felt sermon. When he was sure his compatriots had grasped the essentials of his plan down to the finest detail he stepped down, and the men were led away, the turnkey and the guard with a new and hearty respect for their charges.

Their case was dismissed on Monday, all having told the same story, disavowing that they had ever touched liquor, not only on the night in question, but at any time in their lives. Was not liquor forbidden to them? How then should they obtain it? They were innocent.

"But they were guilty, guilty as sin," Corporal Don Key was heard to mutter as he moved out of the courtroom. "How did they get together so that they could tell the same story?"

The Moose Meaters only smiled serenely and moved quietly out of court.

Nearer My God to Thee

The old man–well not so old at sixty–was on a first class bender. He did not do this often, perhaps two or three times a year; consequently, he felt justified in going on a tear once in a while. As he sometimes explained, it was the only way a healthy man could know what it was like to be without pain. Somehow, his wife was never convinced by this argument.

On this particular day, Steamboat was bleary-eyed and uncertain, but foggy and happy, when he arrived home in the middle of the afternoon. He managed to open the door and stumble in–in fact he tripped on the threshold.

Steamboat laughed at his feet. They did not know where he was going either.

"Get out of my sight, you drunken old bum," shrilled his wife Minerva.

Steamboat did not argue with Minnie, who got downright shrewish whenever he arrived home in inebriated splendour. He was hungry, but he did not dare ask for even a crumb. He was sleepy, but he could not stand still in a room that whirled around in agitated circles.

"Someday that wine is going to kill you," declared Minnie without a trace of pity in her voice. Instead there was, it seemed to George, a hint of a threat, perhaps a wish.

Old Steamboat swooped across the room like a swallow zigzagging to its nest. He fell and giggled as he tried to regain his feet without touching the heavy blankets which were suspended from the ceiling to partition the living room from the connubial bed. He knew from experience that his added weight would bring them down in a heap around him, and renew the vigour of Minnie's wrath.

96

With an exasperated sigh Minnie hauled him erect, thrust the blankets aside, pushed him onto the bed, gave his feet an extra heave, readjusted the drapery, and abandoned him to his fate, tsk-tsking her displeasure.

Steamboat immediately lost consciousness in the pitch blackness.

He awoke to the strains of "What A Friend We Have In Jesus," which wafted into his ears from some outside source. How beautiful it sounded in Ojibway! Old Steamboat, now fully awake, listened, remembering how, in days past, the old people talked in Ojibway.

There was a brief silence. Then "Rock of Ages" filled the air. Old Steamboat felt proud. These Ojibway could sing. Ecstatic, he listened.

"More coffee? More biscuits?" he heard a voice inquire.

Once more the choir resumed singing "Yes, Heaven Is The Prize," the words in Ojibway were haunting, and the choir was the sepulchral best he had ever heard.

God, his people could sing! They could make you cry. That song could make a person weep; the words were deathly. Old Steamboat felt sad, sniffed, felt a tear course down his cheek from the corner of his eye.

Almost without stopping the choir broke into melody, "Nearer My God To Thee."

Why, it was just like a good, old-fashioned wake!

Old Steamboat felt a chill. His throat constricted. He could not see! He shivered in the clutches of a second chill.

Of course it was a wake!–HIS wake. The choir was singing for him. He had died in his sleep just as Minnie had predicted he would someday. He was dead and he was lying, encased and entombed in a coffin. No wonder it was so dark!

He cried silently. He had not even said good-bye to his wife. As he thought, his remorse grew. Why had he not been more solicitous of his wife and his children during his living days? What would God say to him?

God! Old Steamboat quailed in the grip of a frightful fear. He had still to meet his Maker. He still had to be judged!

If only he could go back.

His wife was right, of course. It was the wine.

The choir finished "Nearer My God To Thee."

Old Steamboat heard his wife say, " . . . called the doctor . . . couldn't do anything for him . . . served him right . . . old fool."

Then came a burst of laughter.

Old Steamboat was shocked. Here he was in his coffin, dead, still unjudged, about to be buried, gone forever. Outside his wife was laughing, utterly without sorrow, saying that it served him right. Old Steamboat was appalled. Was this the way it was to be in the end? Must he go unmourned?

He opened his eyes to unrelieved blackness. It was true. He was dead. He tried to move his fingers and felt nothing. Just as he suspected! But God, it was hot! It was not true that the dead were cold–unless–he had heard rumours that hell was a place of fire and brimstone. Not only had the wine finally killed him, it was beginning to look as if his penchant for strong drink had condemned him to everlasting punishment. Was the Lord so unfair as to send him Below without judging him first? Frantically he began to pray. At once a cool breeze fanned his face, and he sighed in relief. If praying slowed his descent so quickly, more petitions ought to assure his place in the hereafter. All that could wait while Steamboat listened to the choir sing his favourite hymn, "Just A Closer Walk With Thee."

Tears welled up again. He stifled a whimper. He did not want to scare those good people who came to say a last farewell to him. People were known to die from heart attacks and seizures brought on by a sudden fright. Not at his wake, he vowed solemnly. Not if he could help it. They didn't know what sorrow was in store for them. Self-righteously Steamboat did not dare to move a muscle.

The song ended.

"Isn't that a beautiful song," his wife was saying, " . . . so peaceful since I put the old Fool in there . . . "

Old Steamboat was horrified. His wife was glad that he had gone to his reward. Once more he shed tears. At the same time he was indignant. Not one tear was she shedding for him; the wife of his bosom showed no grief for the departed, namely him. Such disrespect for the dead! Such a lack of interest in his immortal soul!

Steamboat was enraged. He'd come back to haunt her . . . but on second thought she did not scare easily, and she was sure to nag at him and disparage his supernatural efforts as she had done his earthly endeavours. No, Old Steamboat abandoned the idea of revenge as unbecoming to a ghost of his stature, or a spirit, or whatever he had become.

The choir burst forth with "The Old Rugged Cross."

"They're doing it for me. Good old Minnie got a choir for me. The best singers she could get. All for me."

Old Steamboat forgave his wife her callous disregard for his earthly remains. Once more he wept.

As sobs wracked him, Steamboat endeavoured to stifle all sound bravely, while his head throbbed unmercifully. The choir was singing too lustily. It amazed Steamboat that the dead should suffer human malady.

Blissfully the choir sang on.

Not only did he, a corpse feel pain in his skull, he was hungry. It was most unlike anything he had ever heard about the dead.

The choir sang a joyful "Amen."

"Come on. Let's go," Steamboat heard his wife say to someone. " . . . old skunk . . . be all right . . . "

A door opened, feet scuffled, the door closed. The singing had stopped. He was alone in his coffin, abandoned and friendless.

Once more he gave way to tears. He sobbed loudly this time, no longer holding back.

"To hell with them," he thought.

Suddenly he felt the overwhelming call of nature, the most insistent and imperative of earthly urges, a force irresistible. Frantically Steamboat tried to fight off the urge by squeezing his legs together, but he was unable to overcome the compulsion. As soon as he relaxed his muscles the condition became more intense. In his discomfort Steamboat was mortified. No place to go but in the coffin, and he did not fancy being wet for eternity. Something had to be done, and immediately.

He brought up his arms to push open the lid slowly. He extended them farther, slowly, until he could reach no farther. There was no resistance from above. My God! What did he expect? He, a spirit, could feel no sensation from material things. Experimentally he moved his arms outward. On his right hand was something solid, on his left a fabric. He sat up in the blackness.

His sudden movement sent him lurching against the blankets with which he was encased, snapping the wire that suspended them, and dumped them in a heap on the floor. Steamboat got up, blinking his eyes in the bright sunlight.

On the table was a box he did not recognize. He went over to inspect it. A record player! And on the table beside the machine was a cardboard record casement entitled, "Sacred Hymns Sung by the Rama Reserve Ojibway Choir."

Old Man Steamboat felt good. What an occasion for a celebration.

The Wedding

Forever was happy. He had just asked Bezhinee (Virginia) to marry him, and she had said, "If you wish."

Forever was glad that in these modern times parents no longer selected mates for their children, and that the groom did not have to demonstrate his prowess as a hunter, and his ability to provide for the bride's family as he would have had to do in the old days. Forever had fallen in love, and he was going to marry for love, just like the white people. It was better and happier that way.

Confident that Bezhinee would accept his proposal, Forever had purchased a diamond ring of 1/4 carat proportions, which he now slipped on her finger, moments after she had said, "If you wish." Bezhinee allowed herself the luxury of gazing briefly at the sparkling diamond on her finger before shoving her hand in the pocket of her cardigan. Her fingers constantly explored the unaccustomed outline and hardness of the first ring she had ever owned. She blushed and hung her head down.

That's the way Bezhinee was, bashful.

Forever was different. He was outgoing, cheerful and educated, having spent some seven years in residential school, and thereafter by working in lumber camps. He was a good worker. Moreover he knew what to do at times like this, knowledge wrung from many nights spent at the movies.

"We'll go see the priest on Sunday, after Mass," Forever told Bezhinee, who blushed again.

After Mass on the very next Sunday, Forever led Bezhinee by the hand to the church rectory to see Father Curser, the visiting missionary. Bezhinee trembled. Her hands were cold and damp. Still she went.

Forever knocked on the rectory door.

"Come in," came the muted invitation.

Forever and Bezhinee walked in, closed the door, and stood awkwardly together.

"Come to see you about somepin'" Forever announced, shifting his feet and flashing a subdued smile.

"About what?" asked Father Curser, interrupting the removal of his vestments and looking at Forever suspiciously.

"Me and Bezhineee gotta get married," Forever blurted out. This time his smile was uninhibited.

"Gotta get married!" said Father Curser his eyes narrowing, his visage darkening.

"Yeah," replied Forever. Unaware of the priest's reaction, he was smiling even more broadly.

Father Curser expelled the breath he had been holding and allowed his indignation to bubble over.

"In trouble, eh?" he intoned sarcastically. "You get in trouble and you ask the church to get you out. You're all the same. Get married? You have sinned. You've gone and got this poor girl in trouble. You, Forever. I never expected that from you! Why can't you young people wait and marry for love?" Father had run out of breath.

Forever broke in, "That's right Fauder. We're in love so we gotta get married. Bezhinee here, she don't got no trouble. She's happy her." Father's diatribe had not made much sense to him.

Bezhinee, hearing her name mentioned, hung her head and blushed a deeper hue than before.

"Oh. Oh . . . Well. I'm sorry," Father Curser apologized. "It's just that I never thought . . . that is to say . . . I'm glad, . . . " he trailed off in dismay. "Sit down. And I'll tell you what to do and ask you some questions."

Forever and Bezhinee sat down while Father Curser finished taking off his vestments and hanging them neatly away.

"Now," he said sitting in his comfortable chair, "are you related?"

"Don't think so," Forever replied.

"Well anyway, the people will let us know if there are any impediments after I publish the banns," Father Curser commented jotting down some notes.

"How about totems, Fauder?" Forever broke in. "Bezhinee and me, we belong to the same totem." That had worried Forever before.

"Don't worry about them. They don't mean a thing," said the priest with a wave of his hand, dismissing several thousand years of Ojibway history.

"Now, for some laws of the church ... " and Father Curser outlined the laws governing the marriage act, the duties connected with raising children and the penalties preferred for any infraction of the aforesaid laws.

"You'll need birth and baptismal certificates and a marriage licence," said Father Curser by way of conclusion, after half an hour of explanation. "Do you understand?"

"Yeah, Fauder," Forever said wiping his brow and squeezing Bezhinee's hand.

"Good luck to you both," beamed Father Curser. "Now when would you like to get married?"

"Well,we was thinking about the last Saturday in July, around 10.00 o'clock in the morning," Forever said.

"Let me see," the minister murmured leafing through a well-worn appointment book. "Just fine, nothing else on that day," and he scribbled a reminder.

Turning to the blushing Bezhinee the priest commented, "Ten o'clock. Don't be late, eh? Heh! Heh! Like all the other women." Grasping Forever's hand the priest looked at him sharply. "Heh! Heh! Make sure you show up. Heh!! Heh!"

Forever and Bezhinee left. In the shade of a pine tree by the road, Forever detailed his plans for the wedding as he and Bezhinee sat down.

"Yeah! We'll have a good wedding I'll wear a suit–navy blue –and you'll wear a white gown, something different. Your brother can be best man; your sister can stand up for you. And we'll have a banquet in the Council Hall. I'll buy some wine. I think I can get it cheap from the bootleggers." He paused a moment, and reflected before continuing, pleased with his arrangements, and checking to see if he'd left anything out. "Just like white people. Nobody ever done anything like that around here before. And we'll have a honeymoon, Bezhinee, in the Algonquin Hotel in Sudbury. Ain't gonna stay around here that night with all the noise. Won't be able to sleep."

"What's a honeymoon?" inquired Bezhinee looking and sounding dazed.

"That's going home after the wedding dance all alone and being alone together for the first time and sleeping in the same room ... maybe in the same bed," Forever explained knowingly.

"Why can't we stay home? We can stay at my house. My dad said we can have that house," Bezhinee objected.

"I know. But you know what it's like around here wedding nights," said Forever apprehensively, "Bunch o' guys outside running around the house yelling all night. I wanna sleep. We're gonna be tired. In a hotel be nice and quiet. Nobody bother us."

Bezhinee hung her head down, saying nothing. Forever was pleased.

"Yeah, but my dad can watch. Won't cost so much."

"Huh!" Forever snorted. "Hell, he's the worst one o' them. Get's 'em together you know. And if he's alone, he does it himself."

"But I never been to Sudbury. I don' wanna go," Bezhinee objected.

"Then how'd you like to listen to them guys yelling outside the house," Forever broke in. "And the things they say! 'Did you find it yet? Need any help? Get started yet? Sure you know how? Hey! The house is on fire!' and they keep that up all night. Sometimes they even break into the house, and . . . " Forever didn't finish. Bezhinee blanched.

She was convinced. "Maybe it is better to go to Sudbury," she assented.

During the next two weeks all the preparations were made. The hall was rented by Band Council Resolution. An orchestra was hired. The cooks were engaged. Invitations were sent out. Several cases of Four Aces were delivered–secretly of course–by the local bootlegger. The certificates and marriage licence were secured. Forever bought a new suit, and Bezhinee got her white gown. There was nothing further to do except wait.

The last Saturday of July arrived damply. By 9.00 o'clock Forever was standing with his soon-to-be brother-in-law, Abla-ham (Abraham), and several of his friends on a platform at the rear of the church . A few minutes later Bezhinee and her reti-nue arrived, delivered to the front of the church by a well-dusted 1929 Ford, affectionately known for its roar as B19. There she and her attendants remained, waiting for the arrival of the priest.

At the rear of the church Forever and his companions stood leaning against the walls beneath the eaves, which sheltered them from the drizzle. Forever rolled a cigarette and fidgeted. His companions chatted and joked. As 10.00 o'clock drew closer, Forever extracted the watch from his pocket a little more frequently.

"Priest should be here pretty soon," he observed.

"Don't worry. He'll be here," his colleagues reassured him. "He's never late."

Ten o'clock came and ticked away. Everyone began looking expectantly down the muddy road in the general direction of the highway. Forever rolled another cigarette.

"Wonder where the priest is?" he remarked to Ablaham and the rest of his well-wishers.

"Maybe he had a flat tire," said one of the men.

"Wish it would stop raining. I'm getting wet," Ablaham complained. But no one in the wedding party moved to join the wedding guests who were huddled beneath the trees in the pine grove a few yards from the church.

Eleven o'clock came, but the priest did not. Forever rolled another 'makin's,' looked at his watch anxiously, shook it, held it to his ear, and then sighed. His watch had not flipped its mainspring.

"That priest is late," he complained, squinting his eyes to see farther down the road, hoping to see the car at any moment.

"Maybe he ain't comin'," muttered another voice. Forever hunched his shoulders; that was unthinkable.

"He'd better," the imminent brother-in-law threatened, and he too hunched his shoulders.

"It's clearing up," another said, looking skyward.

"Too late. I'm all wet," said Ablaham. Indeed all of them were wet, their suits baggy from the drizzle.

"Maybe we should phone the priest," suggested Ablaham tentatively.

"Let's wait a few more minutes," Forever urged half-heartedly.

The wedding party stood around silently, making shuffling and coughing noises to cover their apprehension. Rain plopped fitfully from the eaves to the small water-filled depression in which no grass grew.

A little boy ran up. "The ladies say that the meal's ready, almost. Wanna know what you gonna do. Eat now or later." He ran off without waiting for a reply.

Now Forever had to make some decisions. He thought hard.

He turned to Ablaham. "Yeah, I think you should go'n phone the priest. Find out what's the matter."

Ablaham needed no further urging. He ran to the B19. In a few moments the B19, like its famous namesake, roared off.

104

"Hey, Forever! I'm getting hungry." yelled a voice from the pine copse.

"Me too, Me too. Me too," echoed an assenting chorus. "We're all hungry. Come on, let's eat."

"Wait 'til Ablaham gets back," Forever pleaded.

"We bin waiting' fer a long time. Can't wait much longer," one ravenous guest complained.

"Yeah," said a few others bored and discontented. "Might as well go home. Nothing goin' on around here."

Forever was getting exasperated. In fact, he began to long for the good old days when there was a good deal more marriage, and a lot less form and ceremony.

The B19 roared back. The sun began to shine but the air remained uncomfortably muggy.

Ablaham jumped out of the car and walked briskly to the rear of the church, wagging his head negatively as he walked.

"No answer," he said to Forever.

"Maybe we'll eat," Forever said.

Immediately the word spread abroad. "We're going to have the wedding meal," and people began trooping toward the Council Hall, situated across the road from the church.

Twelve o'clock, and still no priest.

The meal was sumptuous; beaver, pickerel, bannock, pies, all the trimmings, all the delicacies, set on tables which had been artfully arranged in a U-shaped fashion.

"Come on Forever. Come on Bezhinee. You go and sit at the head." yelled voices from the crowd. Bride and groom reluctantly went to the head table and sat down.

"Better eat," several ladies suggested to Forever and Bezhinee, who shook their heads in denial.

"Can't. Gotta go to communion," Forever said adamantly, although he was enormously hungry and hugely thirsty. He was a very strict and staunch Catholic. Not even water must pass his lips. He was beginning to doubt the sense of civilized marriage customs and procedures.

"How about some drinks?" a voice boomed out.

"Yeah!" shouted the enthusiastic wedding guests.

Forever looked pained.

Ablaham agree. "May as well have a few drinks; that priest may not show up, and there's no use saving it."

Forever nodded at the inescapable logic in quiet, resigned concurrence. A couple of cases of Four Aces were brought out and the wine bottles passed around. A good number of the men, and some of the women took robust swigs of the "poverty champagne."

One o'clock; no priest. Forever rolled his sixty-fourth cigarette. Bezhinee hardly glanced up.

"Guess it's time to call again," Forever said to Ablaham, who got up quickly and went out.

Shortly he was back with the disconcerting news, "There still ain't any answer."

"Hell, we're gonna miss our bus," Forever complained sadly.

"More wine," a cheerful voice shouted. The mention was immediately seconded by the others. "Yeah, bring on the wine!"

Ablaham opened the fourth and fifth cases of Four Aces and passed out the bottles which went from hand to hand, mouth to mouth. The mood of the wedding guests improved immeasurably. Ablaham sat down, clutching the neck of a bottle. He took a mighty guzzle before depositing the bottle on the floor behind the leg of the table. He was not going to share it with anyone. He grinned.

"How about a toast?" one wag blurted out.

"Yeah, a toast to the woman," burst out another voice.

"The bride," a third voice corrected.

"Yeah! Come on!" Everyone encouraged Forever.

"No, no," objected Forever. "It ain't right." Ablaham took another swig and then stood up. Again he took a healthy gulp, and held the almost empty bottle high. "Hey, you guys. Forever here is gonna marry my little sister. A real good woman my kid sister. Forever, my friend and brother-in-law's a real good man. Them two's gonna make some damn fine couple. Come on! A toast to Mister and Misses," and Ablaham finished his bottle with gusto, tilting his head back and drinking freely. Everyone did likewise, some with wine, some with water.

Ablaham went in search of another bottle to replenish his supply.

"Speech! Speech! Speech!" yelled out many voices in discordant but enthusiastic disharmony.

"No! We ain't married yet," Forever objected, paling at the thought of making even a short speech.

"Come on brother-in-law," encouraged Ablaham opening a new bottle and testing its contents. "You gotta say something. This is all your idea." He went to Forever's chair a little unsteadily, pulled it out, and lifted Forever by the armpits.

"Like Ablaham said, I got a good woman," Forever blurted, and sat back down, patting one of Bezhinee's shoulders. Bezhinee hung her head lower.

The party went on lively and friendly. When the Four Aces was exhausted two more cases of wine were brought out, Slingers this time. Forever had been saving the more potent beverage until the mellow Four Aces had dulled their palates.

"Kept the good stuff until the last, eh?" a voice chided with a laugh.

Forever looked at his watch. It was now 2.00 o'clock and he was desperate.

"Can you phone again?" he asked Ablaham.

"Shore," Ablaham slurred getting up unsteadily. He staggered out. Forever rolled another cigarette, smoked it, and waited. He was hungry but he could not eat. He was thirsty and he wanted to drink, but he could not. When Ablaham had not returned in ten minutes he began to worry.

At 2.30 Ablaham wove an unsteady path into the hall and navigated to the head table as best he could. He sat down heavily, breathing hard.

"No answer," he slurred. "C-C-Called the priest at Blunder Bay too. He used some big word. But it means he can't come anyhow. I even phoned the minister. He won't c-c-come. Don't want to make the b-b-bishop mad. Cheez, Forever, you gotta get married. You c-c-can't have a honeymoon without getting married first."

Forever winced. "Hey, Hon," he begged, "I gotta have a drink. Can I have one? Just a little one?"

Bezhinee shook her head.

"Bring on more wine," said a voice. Immediately some forty odd voices concurred. The remaining three cases of Slingers were opened. The wine bottles were passed around. The party became noisier.

Three o'clock. No priest. Forever asked Ablaham to call again.

Ablaham managed to say, "It ain't my wedding." He took a deep drink and sat back with a beatific smile on his face.

If a call was to be made Forever would have to do it. He excused himself from the table. Outside he found the owner of the B19 whom he persuaded to make yet another trip to the main highway, a mile down the dirt road.

In the store, Forever had to ask permission from the proprietor to use the phone. When this was granted, Forever cranked the handle and put the receiver to his ear.

"Yeah? Who's this?" came a far-away voice faintly over the wire.

"Me. Forever," the groom growled. "Is Father Curser there?"

"Yes. Speaking. What would you like?"

"You were supposed to marry us today. At 10.00 o'clock this morning."

"Oh, my word!" Father Curser gasped. "I completely forgot about it! Went to Sudbury and just got back. Don't do anything. Wait for me. I'll be right there."

Forever restored the receiver to its place. He went back to the hall and gave the good news to Bezhinee, who brightened up at once.

Forever stood up and hailed the celebrants in a loud voice. "The priest will be here inside an hour."

The din did not diminish. No one appeared to hear him. Those drinking kept on drinking; those who were not drinking remained seated and went on talking.

At 3.45 Father Curser drove up in his blue Studebaker coupe, scattering a cloud of dust. He walked briskly to the hall, stopped at the door from where he beckoned Forever and Bezhinee toward the church.

At the priest's motion Forever and Bezhinee got up. Forever glanced back to see if Ablaham could manage alone. Since this appeared doubtful, Forever asked Mike, one of the more sober men to assist Bezhinee's brother to the church. The rest of the crowd followed.

By the time the bride and groom got to the church and took their positions at the front, Father Curser was ready, book in hand. Mike conducted the unsteady Ablaham to his place beside Forever, where he continued to stand supporting the best man lest he fall down.

Father Curser surveyed the motley group in front of him. He bent close to Bezhinee. "Where's your father?" he whispered. "It's his job to give the bride away."

Bezhinee shrugged and studied her shoe.

When word of this fresh disaster spread through the congregation in whispers, several men detached themselves from the crowd and scattered in the hope that Bezhinee's father had not given up and gone home. They returned with him a few minutes later, still drowsy from the excellent afternoon nap he'd been having under the table in the hall. As he was escorted to the front he stifled a huge yawn.

Now the ceremony went smoothly. Bride and groom repeated the solemn and terrifying "I do."

"The ring," Father Curser requested.

"Hey! Ablaham! The ring," Forever asked. "The ring," Mike whispered.

Ablaham twitched his neck, tried unsuccessfully to open his eyes. His head sagged.

"Mike, get the ring from his pocket," Forever whispered. Mike dug into Ablaham's coat. The best man flinched. His eyes shot open glaring at Mike.

"K-Keep your hands out o' my pocket," Ablaham slurred.

"The ring," intoned the priest.

"The ring," Forever pleaded.

"Keep your HANDS out o' my POCKETS, " Ablaham repeated with surly pride. "And KEEP your hands OFF me," he snarled at Mike. "I c-c-can stand up ALONE."

Taking him at his word, Mike let him go. Ablaham's knees buckled. Mike and Forever caught him before he could fall in a heap, and held him erect with difficulty.

Ablaham fished in his own pocket.

"There!" he said. "Got it." But he could remove neither ring nor fist. He struggled briefly. With a yank and a grunt and the sound of tearing cloth Ablaham extracted his fist. There was a flash of gold as the ring flew upward, spinning over the heads of the wedding party. They all clutched vainly at the flying ring. It fell to the floor with a clink of bouncing metal and tinkled down the grate.

Priest, servers, groom, bride, bridal attendant, and Mike, the attendant for the best man got on their knees to study the interior of the grate.

Ablaham sank into a pew, and promptly fell asleep. He snored noisily. Unable to arouse him, the woman beside him used her own unfailing remedy, a kick in the shins. At once his snores subsided, and the good woman nodded with satisfaction.

"What's the hold-up?" came a voice from the back of the church.

"Shshshshshsh!" hissed many voices.

"You must get the ring," said the priest. "You can't get married without a ring. Mike, get some men together and go down stairs. See if you can open that pipe."

As requested Mike vacated the altar area, recruited a small work party from the congregation and went down the steps to the cellar of the church.

Father Curser and the bridal party stood quietly, listening to the heavy breathing of the best man. Father Curser raised his eyebrows at Ablaham's mentor, who again applied her medicine. Again it did not fail. Father Curser nodded.

Violent clanging and whacking sounds echoed through the grate from the basement. There was hammering, tearing, and banging, followed by absolute silence, and then the muffle of voices.

Mike re-entered the church, his coat and hair ash and soot covered.

"No use Fauder. Can't find it. You better borrow somebody's ring."

"Will anyone lend us a ring?" asked Father.

A lady kindly offered her own gold band. With the borrowed ring, the ceremony was concluded without further mishap.

After the service Father Curser apologized contritely.

"Is there anything I can DO," he wanted to know. "I feel that this is all my fault."

"Yeah, Fauder, there is," Forever said. "Me and the Missus here were goin' up to Sudbury for our honeymoon, but we missed our bus now. You can take us."

"Oh my hat! Drive another hundred and fifty miles!" exclaimed Father weakly. "Well, I guess it's the least I can do."

PART 3

GETTING ALONG AND AHEAD OUTSIDE THE RESERVE

How Would You Like Your Eggs?

"Learn English. That's only way you goin' get ahead," some of the elders advised the young. Others added, "It's the only way you can get along with whites; respect you for it." And they would nod wisely, recounting stories of the opportunities they had lost, and the problems they had encountered in support of their recommendations.

Most Indian people did learn English systematically in school or at work, but it made precious little difference. They continued to encounter difficulties in towns and at home. Some of the people became bilingual. However, for many of them, as proficiency in English increased, knowledge of their native tongue diminished. Others, who through disinterest, discouragement, or with a preference for their own first language, avoided English. But since there were white men to be dealt with in ever increasing numbers, that was an impossible situation. For a few, English came accidentally, incidently, and apparently unavoidably.

That was how Ben Cabooge learned English. He did not consider English often. He did not need it; he did not want it. As a fisherman, hunter, trapper, and gatherer of wild rice on Moose Meat Point, Ben got along well enough in Ojibway. On the few occasions that he had had to consort with white people, they were forced to deal with him on his terms. He liked that just fine. But it was not white people who compelled Ben to learn English finally, it was his own people.

One afternoon Ben was mending his nets, when five band members arrived at his cabin. Seeing him hard at work on the rocky shore of the lake, they filed down to talk to him. There were Ezekial Paudash, Pierre Sunigo, George Kaikaik, Chris Choo Chee, and Mary Jane Zeebi. He watched them file their way across the clearing to him. Mary Jane settled herself daintily on a boulder, and the men stood, hands in pockets, watching Ben deftly thread twine through a larger hole.

Ezekial cleared his throat, and came right to the point.

"Ben, we'd like you to run for Council at the elections in July. We need some new blood and some new faces in that Council; be a good thing for the reserve. And you're respected around here."

Ben who had continued to patch the holes in his nets, stopped short. He had never served the band in any capacity before; in fact, he had never entertained such ambitions, and the thought overwhelmed him.

"But I got no experience," he blurted out, his knees growing weak at the thought.

Knowing that Ben would certainly object and give the usual excuses Ezekial had come prepared.

"You don't need no experience. There's enough of us on that Council's got that. Besides fresh ideas are more important than experience any day. You don't have to worry; the agent always helps us anyhow. He knows everything."

Ben had a good mind, quick and logical. Under pressure, his thought patterns accelerated.

"If the agent knows how to do everything, how come he don't do everything himself then? If he knows everything, how come he needs us? And how come we need so many people to run this reserve anyhow? All they do is sit there and talk; waste time."

Ezekial, stumped, scratched his head. He had never looked at band business in quite that manner, had never considered the relationship between talk and action. Maybe it was not such a good idea to ask Ben to serve on the Council after all, if he asked questions like that. Still, having approached Ben, he and his little crowd were duty bound to go through with their enterprise. Besides, things had always been that way, and by God, that was good enough for him. Ezekial recovered his self assurance.

"Ben!" That's the way white people run the country. That's how a democracy works. The Indian Act says we gotta run our own affairs that way," said Ezekial with finality.

Ben was not beaten yet. He knew when to discontinue a particular line of logic and argument, and substitute another. There was, he thought, an infallible way out. Ben took it.

"But I don't speak English," he explained triumphantly.

"I know," Ezekial acknowledged. "You don't have to. Me and a couple of others speak English good. We can interpret things for you. That's what we do for the chief. We figure that you can help us and our reserve or we wouldn't have asked you."

The last appeal was not so easily parried or sloughed off. Since chances of being elected were remote, to avoid offending the petitioners, and to get back to the business of mending his nets while there was still sun left, Ben agreed to allow his name to stand for nomination. He promptly forgot about the election, and went back to the matter at hand.

To his chagrin, Ben was elected, his campaign managers having laboured diligently and well. There was no escape this time. Ben could not withdraw now.

One week after the election, the new Council met to be sworn in and to attend to some immediate business.

Ben took his place at the long table with the other Councillors, the chief, and the Indian Agent. He sat nervously at one end where he hoped he would be inconspicuous. He glanced at his colleagues and at the handful of spectators who had come to watch the proceedings.

A flat brown folder was placed in front of him. He opened it and glanced at the indecipherable and unintelligible marks. He kept it open, but he did not look at it again.

"Mumble, mumble," The Indian Agent was speaking. "Mumble, mumble, grumble," he went on. The speech was as unintelligible as the writing. Ben soon lost the interest that the novelty of the language had generated. Bored, he thought about his fishing.

An assault on his shoulder shook him out of his reverie.

"Raise your hand," his companion hissed in his ear.

"Why?" Ben gasped, startled.

"Raise your hand. We're voting," Ben's friend commanded.

As requested, Ben raised his hand. He was pleased to see that the others all had their right hands raised too. At a nod from the Indian Agent all the Councillors let their upraised arms down. Ben was puzzled by this conduct, but he was glad that being a Councillor was so easy.

"Why do we raise our hands?" he whispered to his friend.

"SHshshshshshshshsh!" The friend put his finger to his lips. "I'll tell you later."

The agent mumbled on. A Councillor was bent over a sheet

of paper writing furiously. From time to time, some of the Councillors spoke in broken, halting English.

"What did he say?" Ben inquired of his companion and mentor, after a particularily emphatic speech.

"Shshshshshsh! I'll tell you after!" responded the friend.

Ben gave up; he began to daydream. His mind went back to his nets and pickerel and whitefish.

"Ben Cabooge, mumble, mumble," the Indian Agent droned.

Ben sat up with a start. He had distinctly heard his name called. He glanced at the scowling Indian Agent. He looked at his unsmiling colleagues. The writer was busy scratching something on the paper. Ben glanced hopefully at the door, but his feet refused to move.

"Mumble, trouble, August 15, mutter, stumble, Ben Cabooge," the agent growled looking at Ben again.

The Councillors put up their hands. Ben shot his arm in the air hoping to make amends for whatever he had or had not done.

"Not you!" his companion said sternly.

Ben was certain he was being expelled from the meeting. That was all right with him. He looked at the secretary hoping for help, but he was recording and could not be bothered to look up.

The Indian Agent grumbled. All the Councillors stood up, including the Agent. They converged on Ben, who was trembling. The chief extended his hand to Ben. Ben took it. They shook hands warmly and vigorously.

"You've just been nominated to attend a leadership conference in London, Ontario, next month," the chief said, smiling.

All the other Councillors including the Indian Agent shook Ben's hand.

"But I don't speak English!" Ben explained again.

"That's O.K." the chief stated. "Indian Affairs will pay for everything. You go by bus, and you'll stay in a hotel. The course will be for one week."

There was nothing for Ben to do but comply. He had to face the inevitable.

The following month, Ben found himself in the London Hotel along with forty other delegates from various parts of Northern and North Western Ontario. An equal number of Indian Affairs officials were to conduct the course.

Somehow Ben checked in without mishap. Well, almost.

116

Ben was uncomfortable, he had to find a toilet. He followed the crowd into the elevator and miraculously arrived at a door whose number matched the one on the key that had been thrust into his hand. His hand trembled as he unlocked the door.

Everything had been done for his comfort. A bed stood in the center of the red-carpeted floor, its padded head resting against a pale wall tastefully decorated with paintings of triumphal arches, and small mirrors. Nice, but no toilet. From a corner flanked by a window, the blank eye of a television set looked at him. Ben almost forgot his discomfort.

Courageously Ben explored a little further. The closet was replete with hangers that clanged at him as he opened the door. Drawers in the bureau and night-stand yielded envelopes, postcards, a phone book, and a bible. Compelled by the strength of a natural need, Ben decided to search on.

Ben opened still another door, this time to the clinical whiteness of the bathroom. At last! But across the seat of the object for which Ben had been searching so avidly, stretched a neat white paper ribbon. What was he to do? If he touched it, he would rip it, and that was unthinkable. He could not tear the decorations that had been prepared so thoughtfully for him.

As he pondered, the door of his room was flung open.

"Ani!" boomed the voice of another delegate. "You all settled? Let's go down and get something to eat. Hey, where's the bathroom?"

Ben indicated the direction with his thumb.

His friend was not so scrupulous as he. Paper was torn and crumbled. So that was how it was done.

That night there was a huge reception, complete with buffet and drinks. Ben nibbled at the unfamiliar food. It was delicious, but all he could think of was the ordeal of the sessions in the morning. A sense of foreboding hung over him like a cloud.

At last he went to his room, and spent a restless, fitful night on the downy mattress.

He was up early the next morning. Finding nothing to do, he sat in the chair and watched the sunrise. He jumped up, stalked to the other chair and looked at the sun from another angle. It would be a good day for fishing he thought wistfully.

Around 8.00 o'clock another delegate knocked on the door, and poked his head inside.

"Bi–weesenin (Come and eat)," he invited.

"I'm not hungry," Ben choked. His stomach growled.

"Come on anyhow!"

Ben reluctantly went down to the cafeteria with his friend.

A large crowd was already assembled in the basement where the cafeteria was located, all the patrons waiting at the foot of the stairway to take their places in the line-up extending the length of the food counter to the cashier's desk. Ben was seized by renewed terror, but, having eaten very lightly the night before, his stomach reproved him loudly. He was hungry. He would have to order food. Realizing that to do so he would have to speak English, Ben broke out in a sweat.

He left the line to observe the proceedings more closely, scan the food, and listen to the waitresses who were shovelling eggs onto plates with lifters. He sidled close to a plump and frumpish waitress who happened to be closest to him. From her, he would learn what was being said, and after he had learned some rudimentary phrases, he would order his food last to avoid embarrassment.

At first the waitress' speech was unintelligible. Fortunately she asked the same question of everyone.

"How would you like your eggs, Sir?"

In reply, some said, "Scrambled," others "Boiled" or "Fried" or "Poached." That did not seem difficult.

After the thirtieth person had gone through the turnstile, Ben had gained confidence. He knew, "How would you like your eggs, Sir?" and "Poached, fried, boiled, and scrambled." He whispered the words silently many times so as not to forget. He made his way to the end of the line repeating the formula to himself. Since he had never eaten scrambled eggs before, and their cheerful yellow colour attracted him, he decided to try some. He repeated, "Scrambled," several more times. He was ready.

No other patron appeared behind him; he was the last. He took a tray. He ambled along, took some cereal, forgoing other selections that were displayed within the glass cases. His mouth watered.

Ben stopped in front of the corpulent, freckled waitress whom he had been observing.

"How, mumble, mutter, grumble, Sir?"

Ben started. This was not what he had learned. The words were unfamiliar.

"Scrambled," he blurted out, not knowing what else to say.

The waitress looked at him in astonishment, a slow smile spreading across her spotted features.

She tried again.

"Scrambled," repeated Ben, running his finger under his collar which had suddenly grown tighter.

This time she giggled. She handed him a plate heaped with fluffy yellow eggs.

Ben took his tray and fled into the dining area.

The waitress turned to her companion.

" How do you like that guy?" she said. "I asked him 'How are you this morning, Sir?' and he said 'Scrambled.' I figured he couldn't hear me so I asked again, and he said the SAME THING."

Her friend burst into peals of laughter. "Boy! We sure get 'em all." she said.

In the dining area Ben savoured every mouthful of the eggs for which he had worked so hard.

Don't Call Me No Name!

Following discharge from the army after World War II, John Meegis (Shell) and his cousin Konauss (Peeling), two Moose Meat Point heroes left the reserve to look for work in London, Ontario. On the day of their arrival, both were hired by a factory and both found lodgings.

After two weeks of labour, both men were paid. With their first pay in their pockets, Meegis and Konauss, assailed by a mighty thirst, went downtown to drink in the bars that they had frequented before going overseas.

It was a hot Friday evening, which, according to the hallowed North American custom of the "week-end," was the best time to drink. Their thirst became overpowering as they came to the Belvedere, a place noted for the geniality of its patrons and its liberality with the laws.

Meegis and Konauss entered with a thirst that had been growing all week. Things had not changed. Floating in the air was the same, blue tobacco smog; the same rancid, sour smell of beer and ale hung about like a miasma; the never-changing rumble of conversation assaulted the ears. God it was good! They found a table bereft of patrons and sat down.

A waiter, perspiration streaming from his brow, came over, carrying a load of empty and full glasses. Meegis and Konauss ostentatiously deposited two two dollar bills upon the table, and licked their dry lips. The waiter seemed unimpressed.

"Indians ain't allowed in here. You'd better leave" he growled.

Meegis and Konauss, flabbergasted momentarily, were speechless. Something had changed after all.

"But we used to come in here, before the war. Used to come in here all the time." Meegis protested without attempting to move.

"I don't care. That was before the war. Forget the war. It's over. Indians is Indians. An' the law says you Indians can't drink."

"How come it was okay for us to drink during the war, an' it's not okay now," Meegis asked, his voice rising. "Jeewus Cwise! How come its okay to fight with you white men, but it's not okay to drink with you guys. Only damn time you people likes Indians is when you need them," and Meegis got up in a threatening manner.

The waiter shouted, "Don't you swear at me. I don't take that from no Indians." At this, all the patrons turned around to stare at Meegis and Konauss. "Get the hell out of here, and don't come back or I'll call the police." The surly waiter walked away.

Dismayed, annoyed, and embarrassed by all the gawking eyes, Meegis and Konauss stalked out. Meegis stopped at the clanging doors, opened them and shouted.

"Go to hell."

As Meegis and Konauss walked away from the Belvedere toward Wellington Street, they found consolation in the fact that London was amply endowed with many fine hotels. They agreed to boycott the Belvedere in the future.

At Meegis' suggestion they went over to the Peridot, a beer parlour well known for bending rules as well as other things. Inside, they sat down and waited for one of the busy waiters to come to them. But no waiter hurried over to take their order. Impatiently Meegis tried one of the civilized customs, learned during his five years of army service. He raised his right arm and snapped his fingers at the waiter.

"Waiter," he called out with authority.

The waiter, a young man with a beer belly and a florid face trundled over to them.

"Two Blue Ribbon," ordered Meegis before the waiter had a chance to speak.

"I'm sorry boys. But we can't serve you," apologized the waiter wagging his head in remorse.

"Jeewus Cwise!" Meegis cursed. "Me and my cousin, we served five years each in the damned army. That makes ten years. An' my cousin here got shot in the leg fighting the white man's war. Can't walk right anymore. He got wounded in the knee in Salerno in Italy, All for you guys. Dammit the hell! Protecting the white man and getting shot should be worth one beer." Meegis, getting angrier at the thought of his cousin's shattered knee, repeated, "Dammit the hell! Next damn time, I ain't goin' to join no damn army. You can fight your own damn wars. This is one Indian who isn't going to believe you people anymore. Promise a better life. Hah. Your damn promises ain't worth anything. We don't ask much, us. Just to come in an' sit down for a beer. Good enough for war, but not good enough for peace. Stick you damn beer up your ear."

But the waiter continued to shake his head in a negative wag.

"I know, but the law's the law. See that sign over there?" he said, pointing to a board, yellowed and fly-specked with antiquity, riveted, nonetheless, to the wall for perpetuity and bearing the soul-shattering inscription, "It is a serious offence for . . . etc," in promulgation of a law passed before the turn of the century, prohibiting the sale and service of spirits to Indians. The laws had been suspended during the war for the benefit of soldiers.

"I'd like to serve you," the waiter continued, "but I'd lose my job and the hotel would be closed down. If the police came in, you'd be arrested."

The waiter retreated, not wishing to prolong the discussion.

"A damned shame," a patron at the next table commiserated.

"Yeah, they should change that law," said another indignantly.

But neither sympathizer offered the men a glass. Meegis and Konauss walked out, still thirsty.

Outside, Konauss suggested, "Let's go to the Iroquois Hotel. Place like that with an Indian name oughta serve us for sure." And they headed in the direction of the Iroquois with renewed hope.

At the doorway of the hotel honouring the Iroquois they met a former comrade-in-arms and his wife. There were handshakes and backslaps, and the invitation to hoist a few.

"Come and drink with us."

Meegis and Konauss, accompanied their friend and his wife into the lounge reserved for "Ladies and Escorts." Never had they been in such elegant quarters. They had heard about the Iroquois Hotel. It had a reputation for propriety. Now, in the company of their white comrade and his wife, they were sure to get a drink. Maybe white people were not so bad after all. Had to meet the right kind. Few and far between.

Inside, they sat down in comfort, thirsty and convivial.

Two of London's beauties, entrenched at the next table, flashing jaded but enticing smiles, extended an invitation to Meegis and Konauss.

"Would you boys like to join us and buy us a drink? We can have a good time."

It was all intoxicating. How good to be in London. Especially at the Iroquois. The girls took their drinks in hands and joined Meegis and Konauss.

The host of the developing party cheerfully hailed a passing waiter. The man smoothed back the non-existent hair on the top of his head, looked at their expectant faces, turned on his heel and disappeared.

Meegis and Konauss gabbled inquiringly with their affable hosts about health and weather, children and work. Reminiscences were bantered back and forth. Meegis had discovered that his new and blond companion answered to the name of Joy, which boded well for the immediate future.

"Boys, you'd better leave," came a stentorian voice. The party looked up. There beside the waiter was an enormous bouncer with a five o'clock shadow no razor would ever efface.

The comrade and his wife protested. "But they're friends. We served together . . . "

"I don't care," thundered the bouncer rudely cutting off the white man and his consort. "Come on boys, move. We can't have you around here."

Meegis and Konauss looked at one another in dismay. Their new-found companions hastily gulped down their beer and retreated from the table.

Meegis and Konauss endured gloomy and inquisitive stares all the way to the street.

Once on the street, Meegis could contain his anger no longer. "Jeewus Cwise, they got everybody in there. Germans. Italians, English, Swedes, and some black men. I even seen a Chinese man. And a couple a' whores. They serve everybody. But they won't serve no Indian. Jeewus Cwise we're gonna get a drink. No goddamned white man is gonna outsmart me. Jeewus Cwise." Having delivered himself of this sermon, Meegis subsided muttering.

The angrier Meegis got, the more determined he became. At the height of his determination, Meegis usually got what he wanted.

Knowing this, Konauss hobbled apprehensively down the street beside his companion.

"Maybe we should put on our battle ribbons and discharge buttons and get our discharge papers," he suggested as he lurched along beside the scowling Meegis.

"May as well throw them away, for all the good they do."

"Won't do no good," replied Meegis with finality.

They came to the Royal Alexandra, where they stood outside for a while, each entertaining the same thoughts, the same doubts.

Meegis was still seething. "Won't serve no Indians," he muttered. "Won't serve no goddamn beer to no Indians."

"Hey Meegis, I been thinking," said Konauss suddenly serious. "You know, you look kinda Chinese."

"Don't call me no names," glowered Meegis pugnaciously.

"No, no, no, no, no. I don't mean it like that. Listen to me. Let's go in there and pretend we're Chinese."

Meegis nodded doubtfully, meaning that he was not averse to the idea as long as it worked.

Meegis and Konauss entered the Royal Alexandra with Konauss shuffling ahead in what he felt was accepted Chinese fashion. They sat down.

A bouncer appeared like a genie.

"We don't serve no Indians here," he barked.

"Don't caw me no name. I not Indian. I Chinee," replied Konauss testily, in his finest Chinese inflection. He arose indignantly.

The bouncer paled.

"Oh, sorry. I'm sorry Sir. Sorry. Didn't mean no insult. Have to be careful you know. Not allowed to serve Indians. Please accept my apologies."

"You bettah," said Konauss, shaking his cane ominously.

"What would you gentleman like?"

"Two Blue Libbon. Pletty damn fast," replied Konauss sitting down.

Meegis and Konauss covered their grins with what they felt were appropriate Chinese bows. They enjoyed their beer vely, vely much.

Good Thing We
Know Them People

With Canada's declaration of war in 1939, all citizens were urged to enlist in the Armed Forces. Those unable to serve in the army, navy, or air force were encouraged to render other patriotic services: scanning the skies for sinister aircraft and reporting the same to some authority somewhere; listening for subversive conversation and relaying the substance to the same unseen authority who was omnipresent in that unknown centre; watching the waters of Porcupine Yellow Liver Lake for unidentified vessels either on the surface or under the water; planting victory gardens; submitting to rationing; cutting down on the use of electricity, and a host of other things. Most particularly, the war effort was to be helped by the collection of scrap metal to be converted into steel and armour plate.

The zealous people of Blunder Bay were fervent and patriotic in the discharge of their duties. They scanned the skies for Stukas and Heinkels, listened for conspiratorial conversation and anxiously surveyed the waters of Porcupine Yellow Liver Lake and Blunder Bay Harbour for periscopes and destroyers. Two thousand, four hundred pairs of eyes watched the skies and waters around Blunder Bay. Two thousand, four hundred pairs of ears were attuned for disloyal whispers or approaching air or water craft.

Like their fellow Canadians, the burghers of Blunder Bay planted victory gardens of liberating squashes, peas, and onions, conserved electricity for the "boys" overseas, and one of their enterprising *entrepreneurs* even collected scrap from the countryside.

From Ashdale to Sputter and Maplewood the scrap man

tracked down load after load of scrap metal; barrel rims, steel barrels, decaying cars, decrepit old tin cans, and rusted barbed wire were items he sought. He even went to the Moose Meat Point Indian Reserve gathering ancient pails, cast iron pots, bent horeshoes, and assorted hunks and chunks of metal.

On these expeditions, the collector would retain one or more Indians to assist him in his patriotic labours.

One of the men so employed was a mute by the name of Herb Codjeesh (Louse). Herb could speak neither English nor Ojibway. He had a speech of his own, partly gestures, partly rudimentary sounds, which only a few friends closest to him could understand. But how the man could work! Moreover, the only remuneration that he expected was a package of Turret tobacco and a booklet of cigarette papers. He would not accept less. For these articles, and for a ride in the back of the truck he would sell his sweat and his muscles for the day. When the work was completed, Herb would get off the truck and go home.

It was the truck driver's custom, on his return from Moose Meat Point with a load of scrap metal, to stop off at the Algonquin Hotel in Blunder Bay for a couple of cold beers. Gathering metal for the war effort was hot work, deserving of reward. On this particular day the driver left his truck still full of scrap parked outside, and went to his reward with several friends.

He joined the patrons of the Algonquin drinking their beer and welcoming the boys in uniform who were home on furlough. A little later, one of the local Onion Valley farmers, eyes bulging, face flushed, poked his head in the door.

"Hey, we just captured a Japanese spy," he belched excitedly.

The drinkers were thunderstruck.

But the truck driver, with his wits about him called out, "Where?"

"Down by Smith's," affirmed the denizen of Onion Valley.

"Who caught him?" inquired an inebriated soldier getting unsteadily to his feet. Something more seemed to be required of him because of his uniform. But because both his legs and his imagination failed him, he sat back down.

"A couple a' guys from Blunder Bay," said the informant.

"Did anyone call the police?" asked another voice.

"Yeah, but he's not around–his day off," came the intelligence.

"O.K., so who's holding him?" an anxious voice inquired.

"There's some soldiers out there got ahold of him. They're taking him to jail, and they're calling the Mounties."

126

The Onion Valley farmer dragged himself into the hotel. The patrons gathered around him reluctant to move out. Drinking was forgotten.

"What was that spy doing?" someone wanted to know.

"Why, he was walking up the street as bold as brass, talking Japanese and saluting."

"Holy Smokes!" uttered an astonished chorus of voices.

"And he was wearing a Canadian Army uniform with all the badges," added the farmer, nodding his head.

"Let's go and see!" a voice suggested.

Agitated and excited, the drinkers moved out onto the street.

Main Street was dotted with small groups of people gabbling excitedly. The atmosphere in Blunder Bay was electric and uneasy.

"Wearing the uniform of a Canadian soldier. That's against the rules of war," a distraught voice wailed.

"Yeah, it's fiendish," agreed another.

The truck driver and his cronies moved along past Cass' Pool Hall and a hardware store. They stopped at another small group to inquire of one another, "Where did he come from?"

"Some people say that he must of got off a submarine. There's a bunch gone down to the docks to check the bay," replied an informed source.

"Maybe he parachuted down," offered another.

Everyone checked aloft to make sure this was not part of an invasion, but the skies contained neither cloud, nor plane, nor parachute. Reassured, they continued their conversation.

"I'll bet there's more of them. You know they never work alone," said a frumpish woman articulating the fear that was spreading among them.

Several looked at the people around them with narrowed eyes. A person could never be too careful of who stood beside him in these uncertain times.

The truck driver's crowd moved on, listening to the buzz of conversation.

"Did anyone get in touch with the army," a man inquired querulously.

"Yeah, I think the Blunder Bay Bugle man got on the phone."

"Mebee they'll send the army," sighed a nervous but hopeful citizen.

Almost everyone was moving down the street toward the large crowd standing outside the jail-house door.

"By God, these guys think of everything. Who but the Japanese would think of landing near an Indian reserve. Damned hard to tell them apart you know. Same hair, same colour, same slant to their eyes. You never know," came an ominous observation.

"Yeah; they say the guy was talking sumping like one of those Indians from Moose Meat Point. Cheez, they think of everything," moaned another vigilante.

"Damned good thing we know all them people from Moose Meat Point, or we'd really by fooled."

The little crowd around the truck driver was at the doorway ready to enter. A Moose Meat Point soldier on leave, just arrived in town, joined them.

"What's going on?" he asked of the truck driver.

"We captured a Japanese spy, just a while ago. He's in the cell now. We're going to see him."

"Holy Smokes!" remarked the soldier as he joined the crowd waiting to see Blunder Bay's spy.

While they were waiting, the truck driver gave the run down to Moose Meater, who scratched his head thoughtfully as he remarked, "Guess they'll have to shoot him."

Momentary silence ensued while this observation was digested. Then the remark was whipped out of the jail-house like lightning on the tongues of the vigilantes.

"There's going to be an execution! A firing squad!"

Everyone was excited at the prospect.

"Where?" asked a little old lady, her black hat bobbing with indignation. "When?"

No one knew.

Truck driver and Moose Meater were at the cell door, which contained a barred square window at the top and a barred vent at the bottom, some four inches from the floor. Unable to see the prisoner through the aperture at the top, truck driver and Moose Meater got down on their knees to inspect his appearance from the bottom. The prisoner of war was looking back at them from the same opening.

The truck driver got up first, his face once flushed had turned ashen.

"My God! It's my helper from Moose Meat Point, Herb Codjeesh."

Moose Meater remained bent over, holding his sides to prevent himself bursting from laughter.

Outside, the little old lady, her black hat bobbing in disappointment muttered "There ain't gonna be no execution."

The spy, captured by the burghers of Blunder Bay was the mute Indian from Moose Meat Point who had, dressed in an army outfit given to him by the soldiers of his community, stowed away in the scrap salvage truck.

It took a priest, an Indian Agent, a minister, his mother, brothers, and several other personages to vouch for his identity and to secure his release from the reluctant authorities.

They Don't Want No Indians

The phone rang.

"Yes. Sudbury Indian Centre!" Zubyaeh (Xavier) barked in his ordinary gruff voice.

"I'd like to speak to Mr. Xavier McMac," a tinny voice grated in his ear.

"Speaking! Who's this?" Zubyaeh growled.

"Yes. It's Sergeant Goodenough of the City police."

Zubyaeh examined his conscience briefly and discovered no personal sin against society.

"O.K. What can I do for you?" he asked curtly.

"Well, we have an unidentified body at the City Morgue here. Hard to tell whether he's Indian, Chinese, Japanese, or Korean, but he could be one of your people. I've been trying to locate someone who might know him and frankly, Mr. McMac, I've drawn a complete blank. You know all the Indian people around town, so I thought perhaps you could help me. Can you come over?"

"Right," snapped Zubyaeh. "I'm on my way."

With one motion he put down the receiver and grabbed his coat.

"Goin' to the Morgue," he boomed out to the office in general, as he made for the door.

Heads snapped up. Startled eyes watched his exit.

Zubyaeh, unaware of the consternation he had left behind, reached the Morgue in record time.

Was it his imagination, or did the damp bite of formaldehyde assault his nostrils as he walked in? Zubyaeh shuddered but walked briskly to the reception desk.

"What can I do for you, Sir?" the little receptionist asked sweetly.

"Sergeant Goodenough asked me to come over to identify a body," Zubyaeh rumbled, squaring his shoulders, and glaring.

Zubyaeh was always a gruff, no-nonsense person. His unsettling errand gave him an air of cold detachment as well. At his frown the little receptionist paled.

"One moment, Sir!" she quaked, and scurried around the corner behind her desk.

She returned immediately.

"Sergeant Goodenough, Sir!" Introductions completed, she resumed her duties.

"Mr. McMac?" the huge uniformed man asked with uncertainty.

They shook hands.

"Yeah, that's me," Zubyaeh pumped the man's hand twice, and dropped it abruptly. "Where's the body?"

The officer led the way into a cold inner sanctum, where a white-smocked attendant beckoned them both to a hospital bed at the end of the room. He pulled back a white sheet that covered the corpse. Zubyaeh looked.

"Why, it's Dan Pine Cone," said Zubyaeh, "from Moose Meat Point but now registered on the Ishpiming Reservation." He flicked away a tear that collected in the corner of his eye. Zubyaeh was always deeply affected by the death of someone he knew.

Officer Goodenough waited a few moments out of deference, while Zubyaeh reflected on the mortality of men and the lonely death of this man in particular. But Zubyaeh was a practical man. There were things to be done. He pulled his thoughts back to the present and the matters at hand.

"Does he have any near relatives?" asked Sergeant Goodenough.

"Yeah. There's his wife. She's in town somewhere. But they've been separated for years. She's white, you know," explained Zubyaeh.

"Do you think you can locate her?" the officer inquired.

"Well, I can try. Can't promise anything. She liked to move around some, that woman."

"Good," said Sergeant Goodenough with a sigh of relief as they headed for the door. "We'll wait for you to contact us."

Several days of diligent detective work failed to turn up Myrtle, the wife of the deceased. Zubyaeh then remembered

Myrtle's habits and began to search the Sudbury taverns. Sure enough, an afternoon of pub crawling ran Myrtle to earth.

Zubyaeh broke the news as gently as he could.

Myrtle promptly burst into slightly alcoholic tears.

"Oh, my dear, dear Dan, my dearest Dan, my darling," she sobbed, startling the patrons, several of whom began to cry in sympathy. She moaned; she sobbed; she wound her sturdy arms around her ample bosom.

Seldom had Zubyaeh seen such a display of grief. He too, swallowed hard against the lump in his throat.

"Come on Myrtle," he said gently, taking her by the elbow. Myrtle got up shakily, and allowed herself to be led out.

Myrtle broke into fresh tears at the sight of her husband's body in the Morgue.

"Yes that's him. It's Dan. My poor dear Dan," she sobbed. Had Zubyaeh not held her back, she would have thrown herself across the still form.

Sergeant Goodenough and the attendant scribbled something on a sheet of paper, relief mirrored in their faces.

"Now, Mrs. Pine Cone, you can claim the body for burial," the officer said kindly. "You can arrange the transfer of the deceased to a funeral home."

"But I ain't got no money," wailed Myrtle. She stopped suddenly in mid-sob. "He ain't got any insurance either, I bet."

It was a sobering thought. Myrtle began to edge toward the door.

"Mr. McMac, can you make arrangements?" the attendant asked.

"Yeah! What do I have to do?"

Myrtle came forward again to listen.

"First, of course, there's the charge for the storage of the body. That's gotta be paid. Then you get the wife here to sign a form releasing the body to you. Once that's done the body's yours. Do you understand?"

"How much?" Zubyaeh asked, eyes narrow.

The attendant frowned, making mental calculations.

"Been here five days," he muttered, "Be a hundred dollars."

Zubyaeh raised his eyebrows. "I'll see what I can do."

He went out, stopped, poked his head back around the corner.

"Myrtle, you sign those release forms, you hear?"

Myrtle nodded dolefully.

Zubyaeh went straight to the offices of the District Supervisor of Indian Affairs, a Mr. Whipple-Baxter. He came to the reason for his visit at once.

"Mr. Whipple-Baxter, there's a dead Indian over there at the Morgue, Dan Pine Cone. Morgue wants a hundred dollars before they can release the body. Since he's from Ishpiming, a registered Indian, and his wife's got no money, can you people pay the storage? He deserves a decent burial on his own reserve. I can take his body up after it is released."

"One moment now, Mr. McMac. Of course we'd like to help, but you know our position. Once an Indian leaves the reserve, whether or not he's registered, he becomes the responsibility of the province. He's no longer our responsibility. It's about time the province assumed some of the responsibility for its own citizens."

"Listen," Zubyaeh interrupted the District Supervisor, with a menacing index finger pointed directly at the man's nose. Such was the force of Zubyaeh's personality that, although many feet separated them, the man moved a step backward. "I didn't come here to hear about policies. I know all about your goddam policies. I want a hundred dollars for the release of Dan Pine Cone so's he can get buried on his reserve. Can you give me the money? Yes, or No."

"I can't."

"Yes or NO!" snarled Zubyaeh pounding a fist on the desk. "I don't want to know what you can or can't do. Will you, or won't you?"

"No. Mr. McMac, be reasonable. I can't."

"O.K. That's better. Why didn't you say so before instead of wasting my time. You're supposed to help Indians, not work against them. You won't help the live ones, and, by God, you won't help the dead ones either. Indian Affairs–Hah! You're no bloody help at all."

Zubyaeh slammed the door behind him.

He was angry, and getting angrier. Zubyaeh jumped into his car. He drove as if he hated his car, other cars, pedestrians, traffic lights, and above all the Traffic Act, which like other laws was made for the hindrance and nuisance of honest citizens, and affected dishonest citizens not at all. In this state he roared up to the District Office of the Provincial Department of Health and Welfare, and screeched to a halt in front.

Zubyaeh bounded up the steps of the building in a manner befitting his decisiveness. Except for the strength of the doors, he might have broken them down by the force of his entry.

"May I help you sir?" asked a pallid nondescript young thing.

"I want to see the supervisor," bit off Zubyaeh, his eyes flashing harpoons.

"Wh-wh-which one sir?" stuttered the startled girl.

"What do you mean which one? How many you got anyhow? ANYONE. Just get me one. You hear? ANYONE. But one!" Zubyaeh bellowed.

"B-b-but I need a name before I can help you, sir," she stammered.

Zubyaeh settled down somewhat. "Get me anyone," he repeated, "I don't give one whit what they're called. It's an emergency. It's a matter of death."

At the mention of death the little receptionist scurried away. She came back quickly with a scrawny old matron in grey, her hair secured in a bun on the top of her head with enormous bobby pins.

"Mrs. Pukey-Baker" announced the girl and scurried away.

Zubyaeh eyed her with disfavour. "I'm Xavier McMac from the Indian Centre. There's a dead Indian at the City Morgue. They want a hundred dollars to release him. He's from Ishpiming and he ought to get buried there. His wife has no money."

"I'm sorry Mr. McMac. That's not our business. You should go to Indian Affairs. It's their responsibility not ours . . . "

Zubyaeh answered with all the dignity he could muster. "I have just come from Indian Affairs. They sent me to you. They say that it's your responsibility. You people are passing the buck. This man needs help."

"Mr. McMac, I'm afraid Indian Affairs is neglecting its responsibilities. It is the law, and it is policy. The province cannot encroach on federal affairs."

"Oh, Dammit!" Zubyaeh exploded. "You guys are just like Indian Affairs, making all kinds of excuses, giving no help, hiding behind jurisdiction. You want Indians to integrate, then you don't want them to. Nobody wants them; nobody wants us." Zubyaeh became bitter. "What do you do around here all day, anyhow, except make excuses. Won't even try to help a poor Indian, and a dead one at that. No use talking to you people."

Finished with his tirade, Zubyaeh stalked out, leaving Mrs. Pukey-Baker flushed, lower lip quivering.

Zubyaeh was not beaten yet. But what to do? Back in his own office he grabbed the phone to call the Ishpiming. Then he remembered that the Ishpiming Band Office had no phone, and with an exclamation of disgust and impatience he called his bank to arrange a small loan. The request was granted with no questions asked, which was just as well. How could he explain that he was about to get a dead Indian out of hock with the money? Half an hour later, the money in his pocket, Zubyaeh drove to the Morgue.

Myrtle had signed the paper releasing the body to Zubyaeh for burial, and was back at her accustomed habitat drowning her sorrows. With the payment of the money Zubyaeh was free to take the corpse. He was relieved, exultant at the thought that, with only his wits to guide him, he had been able to extract a body from the clutches of the law, in spite of the impediments of all departments of the government. And Dan Pine Cone would feel the same he was sure. It was the best send off a man could have.

Transport for the body to Ishpiming still had to be arranged, and not, his measuring eye told him, by car. Nor, now that the release of the body had been accomplished, was he inclined to go alone. He resolved to borrow a small truck, and invite one or two friends to accompany him. The nature of their cargo would be his secret. It was better so.

He persuaded a couple, Bob and Hortense, to travel with him on the promise that they would return that very night. The three of them set out the same afternoon in a small, half-ton truck on loan from a friend. Zubyaeh had picked up the earthly remains of Bob Pine Cone first, and wrapped him in blankets since no casket, coffin, or even a rough box was available. Tenderly he placed the body in the back. Dan had sometimes travelled that way in life, and would not have objected to such a ride after death, Zubyaeh was sure.

The drive along Highway #144 to Gogama was pleasant. From Gogama to Ishpiming, the road, owned, maintained, and used by a lumber company was rough, replete with hills, gullies, bumps and curves, and just wide enough to admit the passage of one vehicle in the summer. Along this tortuous route Zubyaeh held the wheel in unnatural silence. He cast surreptitious glances in the rear-view mirror as they bounced along. Sometimes, on the worst of the ruts, he held his breath, and said a small prayer that his cargo might arrive intact. But all seemed well in the back of the truck.

"You're not saying much," Hortense observed glancing at Zubyaeh, whose jaw was set in anxiety.

Zubyaeh unlocked his teeth. "Just thinking."

Silence extended over the trio. The bumps, hollows, and potholes grew worse, "like a wash-board" thought Zubyaeh, as he gripped the wheel. The effort of keeping the truck on the road, and at a reasonable speed made his knuckles turn white.

One massive jolt followed by a shotgun-like explosion stunned them all.

"Dammit the hell," Zubyaeh muttered. "We busted a tire and no place to park on the road." The truck cluttered and bumped as Zubyaeh guided it along.

Hortense, who had been half turned in her seat to ease the discomfort, noticed movement in the back window from the corner of her eye. She turned and stared through the back window.

"Why," she exclaimed, "it's Dan Pine Cone. You didn't say he was coming with us. And he's gone to sleep sitting up. I sure don't know how he managed it on this road. He'll get cold back there, Zubyaeh, We can make room for him up here."

Zubyaeh shot an agonized glance in the rear-view mirror. Sure enough, the corpse, now in an upright position, sank slowly down again. Zubyaeh gulped, and swallowed hard.

Hortense had been watching too. "Oh, Zubyaeh! He's sick! Stop! He needs help!" she cried.

"Can't help him now," ground out Zubyaeh keeping his eyes on the road.

"Why not?" inquired Bob doubtfully, with the presentiment that something was not as it should be.

"Well, I didn't want to scare you any. Figured you'd find out after, and it'd be O.K. Dan's dead and I'm taking him home for a proper burial," explained Zubyaeh sheepishly.

"God!" gasped Bob.

"I think I'm going to be sick," quavered Hortense.

"Don't you dare!" Zubyaeh gritted. "We got enough troubles as it is."

He manoeuvred the truck onto a grassy verge, where he brought it to a careful halt. Behind them the dust of their passage settled slowly back to the road-bed.

Zubyaeh reached for the handle of the door.

"You're not leaving me alone in here!" wailed Hortense in a paroxysm of terror.

"You can hold the flash-light," said Zubyaeh kindly.

It was hard for Zubyaeh to crawl in the back, past the

earthly remains of Dan Pine Cone, to reach the spare tire and the jack; harder still to change the tire by the flickering light of the flash-light held in Hortense's unsteady hand. Bob watched the back of the truck as if it were full of rattlesnakes. Hortense moaned softly to herself from time to time. Somehow the task was completed.

After he had returned the tools and the deflated tire to the back of the truck, Zubyaeh straightened the blankets on his erstwhile friend. With a pat of apology for the indignities he had inflicted on Dan's mortal shell, Zubyaeh muttered, "Hang in there, old fellow. It's the only way to get you home."

Back in the truck and underway once more, Bob and Hortense gripped one another for support. Both glanced back often. The trip was completed in awkward silence.

Nearing the end of the trip, Zubyaeh reflected that he had given no thought to what he would do with the body once he arrived. Accordingly, he stopped at the local detachment of the O.P.P. for guidance.

"Impossible!" shouted the appalled O.P.P. Sergeant. "There's no room for . . . for . . . " and he broke off shivering. Modulating his surprise and his voice he tried again. "We aren't set up to handle bodies. Take him . . . it . . . whatever . . . out of here!"

"What in the hell do you expect me to do with him then?" glowered Zubyaeh.

"That's your problem. You brought him in here."

Zubyaeh felt his gorge rise. "Yeah," he snarled, "It figures. Just like the damned government. Only time you guys show up is when there's trouble. O.K. We got trouble now. So what about some help for a change?"

The initial request had nonplussed the officer, but he was recovering rapidly.

"Listen Mr. McMac. Do you have a mortician's licence?"

"No. Why?" Zubyaeh was puzzled.

"Because if you don't get that body out of here, I'll charge you with an offence contravening the Mortician's Act. What's more, if you don't stop shouting, and abusing us, I'll charge you with disturbing the peace."

And the officer meant it.

For the first time in his life Zubyaeh was speechless.

"Why don't you take the body to the priest?" the officer suggested.

"Yeah, that's a good idea. Never thought of that. Thanks."

Zubyaeh and his cohorts left the police station and approached the residence of the priest. But the priest was in Sudbury according to his housekeeper, and would not be back for several days.

Zubyaeh explained his predicament.

"Can I leave the body here for the night, then?" he asked.

"Mary, Joseph, Jesus, No!" the woman closed the door abruptly in their faces. It was dark.

"Oh, let's try the minister," pleaded the distraught Hortense. "I'm not going to drive around all night with Dan's corpse in the back. It wouldn't be so bad if he'd lie still, but he keeps sitting up once in awhile. Please, Zubyaeh. Dan wouldn't mind where he slept if he was alive."

There was truth and sense in what Hortense said.

A tall, thin clergyman answered the knock at the rectory door.

"Good evening," he drawled.

Zubyaeh told him graphically why it was not a good evening for the shivering trio.

The minister's eyebrows shot up to his receding hairline. "Is ... that is, was he Catholic?" he asked.

"Yes, he was." Zubyaeh was sure of another rejection.

"You know that we are Anglicans. Whyever would you wish to leave him here?" questioned the minister, fighting the astonishment that almost overwhelmed him.

"Seems to me you guys say 'We're all brothers in Christ,' so I figured maybe you'd help out some."

"Actually, my dear fellow, that is the spirit of the Christian Church. But surely the deceased would rest more comfortably with those of his professed religion." On droned the minister warming to the theme of brotherhood and all that it implied. He ended on a negative note. "Surely you can see why I think you should take him to the priest."

"He's not there, and his housekeeper's a flighty old bat. Closed the door on us."

"I really don't think ... " began the minister.

"Oh do be sensible Oscar," spoke up his wife who had drifted quietly to his side and had heard most to the exchange. It pleased her to overrule her husband on occasion, lest he get above himself. "See how far these good people have come. What difficulties they have overcome in the name of brotherly love. We could well learn a lesson from what has transpired. Only think, my dear, what a fine sermon this would make for Sunday."

Oscar listened, and was impressed. The idea had merit.

"Yes, I see. Very well. Bring the body in."

Zubyaeh had been looking back and forth from one to the other in astonishment, and without much hope. He needed no second invitation to act.

"Come on Bob," he said in jubilation, his purpose almost accomplished.

But Bob stood rooted to the spot.

"Oh, no. Zubyaeh. No thanks. Didn't say I'd carry any bodies around for you when I came. You go ahead if you want. I'm staying right here."

Zubyaeh looked hopefully at Hortense, who buried her head in the front of Bob's jacket and refused to look back at him.

"Come along," said the minister poking his head around the corner of the door. "We've found a suitable place for the remains in my downstairs study. I trust that will meet with your approval."

"Well, you see, Reverend, I can't move him by myself, and Bob here has turned chicken . . . "

Bob refused to rise to the insult.

"Very well. Very well," the minister sighed.

After he had wrapped the body of his friend once more, Zubyaeh with the help of the minister, took a firm grip on the corpse, and staggered up the walk and through the door with their burden that had grown exceedingly heavy. The relief with which they deposited it on a small roll-away couch in the book lined study was heartfelt. Zubyaeh felt the burden lift from him at last.

"Thanks a lot, Reverend," said Zubyaeh, and pumped the hand of his confederate with relief.

"Won't you stay for coffee, against your journeys?" asked the minister kindly. "My wife and I would like to hear what brought you to such a pass."

Zubyaeh accepted gratefully. Bob and Hortense refused, and remained huddled in the truck, consoling one another.

After Zubyaeh had consumed several cups of excellent coffee, and told the minister and his wife all they wished to know, he shook Oscar's hand more warmly than ever, promised to drop in again when he was in the vicinity, and went whistling out to the truck.

Bob and Hortense regarded him round-eyed but without rancour, and he smiled at them.

"You see?" he said. "Just keep at a thing and by God you get it done one way or the other."

Can I See the President?

"Did you get a job?" my landlady inquired with a laugh of greeting as I stepped into the house.

"No, I didn't," I replied with an equal amount of cheer. What a startling revelation that I was expected to be job hunting! Work was absent even from my innermost thoughts at the time. I had enough money to pay for room and board for a couple of weeks, and to sustain me in leisure for a while longer if I was careful, before I was ready to seek employment. Nothing, I determined, was going to prevent me from enjoying a holiday, which I felt I deserved after having worked and studied for six years without a holiday.

But several days later, returning to the house, I encountered the landlady's daughter at the door. She was on her way out, and paused only long enough for her to spew out her usual venomous pleasantries.

"Still unemployed!" she remarked tartly. "Humph!" Her acid snort reverberated from the walls. "Lazy! Just like the rest of the Indians."

Neither her mood nor her tone immediately disturbed me. She was, in any event, naturally sour by disposition and appearance. Our brief meetings had shown me the most effective way of emerging the victor.

"I could go for you," I countered, with what I hoped was a lewd grin, knowing that such sentiments would be insufferable to her.

"Ah, nuts!" the Twit said with disgust, glared, and stomped out.

Although I was pleased with the reaction, I was disturbed

by her taunt and the implication of her remarks. I knew that the money I had would soon be exhausted, forcing me to look for a job shortly. The last thing I wanted was for her to think that she was in any way responsible for my efforts in job hunting, coming as they were about to, on the heels of her comments about my worth. She must not think that I had yielded. But reviewing my dwindling finances, I knew that I really had no choice. Twit had me over a barrel.

For several days I scanned the "Help Wanted" columns in the *Globe and Mail*, the *Daily Star*, and the pink-paged *Telegram*; then I began to study them in earnest. I had to know what positions were available and what was required of job applicants.

With a fairly new B.A. and a capacity for hard work, I did not anticipate much difficulty in finding suitable work.

Right from the beginning I began to encounter impediments. For one thing the advertisers had a remarkable facility and ingenious perversity for ambiguity and obscurity. The terms they used did not mean what they seemed to mean. With the aid of a dictionary and by making discreet inquiries, I soon learned what Tree Surgery, Sanitary Engineering, Traffic Management, Expediting, and other similar terms meant.

Other equally equivocal terms were not so easy to understand, except through hard experience. After applying for a public relations position with the Pleasant Meadows Memorial Gardens Corporation, I began to distrust all advertisements, concluding that public relations was the art of making bad things look good.

That I was not hired to peddle the austere splendour of cute little funeral urns owed more to good fortune than to my powers of resistance. When the very persuasive gentleman who was interviewing me, absented himself for a moment, I bolted to the sanctuary of the open streets at Yonge and Eglinton.

I did soon discover that my previous experiences of fishing, hunting, lumberjacking, mining, and farming were of little worth and no consequence in relation to employment in the city.

Nor as it turned out had I a clear idea as to a specific career to pursue. Earlier, I had determined upon a career in law, and I had considered no alternative. Consequently, when I failed Torts, Land Law, Contracts, indeed every law thrown my way, I had to reassess my ambitions and the careers available.

After the initial disappointment at my failure to pass the

law course, I concluded that it was a good thing—good for tort-feasors, wife-beaters, chisellers, and an assortment of other offenders, great and small, who might have sought to retain my services as counsel that I might extricate them from their entanglements with the law. Willing I would have been, but successful . . . ?

Thus having been abandoned by the law, I was at a serious disadvantage since no other profession especially appealed to me. Again "Help Wanted" provided a basic idea for a career, "Personnel Relations." Just what I wanted.

I was ready to offer my services to any corporation that was interested in my help on a week's notice. On Sunday night I resolved to sally out next morning to look for a position in earnest. I planned to begin with the smaller buildings on Bloor, and work my way down to Yonge and King.

Monday morning I was up before the pigeons. After showering, I put on my finest coat, pants, white shirt, and tie. Frantically I shined my shoes. Just before stepping out of the house I made one final check in the mirror, to make sure that my tie was straight, and the Brylcreem had performed its wonders for my hair. A second look convinced me that no matter what I tried to do to my appearance, I could not improve God's handiwork. I was as presentable as possible.

According to my plan I began my walk from Queen along Parliament up toward Bloor Street. I walked slowly to organize my thoughts on the best possible approach in addressing the president of a large corporation.

"Mr. President," I practised, "my name is Basil Johnston." Here I would offer my hand, and take his, shaking it vigorously. "I am desirous of obtaining a position in your Personnel Relations Department and becoming a member of your esteemed organization which I know by reputation to be the kind with which I would be proud to be associated."

I mouthed the words and the sentences several times. The texture! The tone! The harmony! Surely the president would be impressed by my command of English. I repeated the sentences several more times. But with each rendition, their authority and charm and melody diminished proportionately. Something told me that such an approach was not quite appropriate. Quickly I rejected the entire speech.

"Mr. President," thought I, trying another method, "Good morning." At this point I would offer my hand in greeting and salutation, and vigorously pump the president's hand. "How do you do?"

I was cheered and encouraged. I walked a little more briskly. Just the way white people greeted one another! Why had I not thought of it before? It was friendly and compassionate, two attributes that would warm any president to my charm and good manners.

But what did those words mean? I considered. Incomprehensible, they defied all sense. Substituting, "How are you?" was no better. I slowed down, wondering if, in fact "How are you?" had any meaning, since it was asked indiscriminately of the sick and the healthy alike. I dismissed the approach as unsuitable.

I began to develop a chill, and broke out in goose-pimples while perspiring. How was the eminence of an *entrepreneur* to be addressed? How was one to deport oneself in the august presence of a Board Chairman?

I was certain of one thing; presidents and their kind were unlike lumber camp foremen, mine shift bosses, farmers, and fishermen. With the former I suspected a circumspect approach; with the latter all that was required or expected was either, "Do you need a man?" or "I'm looking for work." If work were available they would ask, "Can you work?" To such a question the job applicant replied either, "Yeah," or "Damn right," with as much authority as his stature would allow. It was all so simple. Why was business not like that? Why did it have to be so confoundedly complicated?

Not wishing to go any further, I went into a restaurant at the corner of Parliament and Wellesley Streets to collect my thoughts and reconsider the situation further. I sat down somewhat morosely.

"Whadayawan?" rasped the scruffier of the two waitresses reluctantly getting up from her bench in a booth and snuffing her cigarette in the ash tray, already piled high with burnt offerings.

"Coffee," I managed to croak.

I watched her fill the cup with an evil, muddy black substance which I presumed was coffee. She set the mug down in front of me with such hostility that some of the coffee splattered over the rim.

"These foreigners never say thank you when you serve them," she complained to a companion, "especially the Chinks."

My earnest study of the premises turned up neither foreigner nor Chinese. Since I was alone, I concluded that she meant me. But I had greater troubles than a frowzy, ignorant, and, from the look of her, unwashed female.

The coffee tasted as bad as it looked. Thoroughly discouraged I considered abandoning the employment quest for the day. Then I remembered Twit, and I could not go back. Either I had to continue until I found employment and so confound her, or remain unemployed and confirm her beliefs about Indians. Twit had me over TWO barrels. I chose the lesser of two evils.

When I had finished my coffee, I reluctantly made my way up Parliament, turned westward along Bloor to Yonge Street. At the corner of Bloor and Yonge I paused for another coffee to reinvigorate my faltering resolution. I felt a little better realizing that by the time I got down to the vicinity of Bay and King, I would have had enough experience gained along the way in the smaller buildings to enable me to speak with some confidence to the great and reputed scions of industry, in the larger buildings.

I had walked only three or four blocks when I perceived what I was looking for. I did not have to go any further. My heart thumped; my knees got weak as I gazed admiringly at the great diamond-shaped billboard, yellow neon lights running clockwise in perpetual motion around "The Goodyear Tire and Rubber Company Ltd."

From the northeast corner of Yonge Street I continued to gaze at the sign, the emblem of MY company, the name that had once graced the crest of a hockey club, "The New Toronto Goodyears." My excitement mounted.

My immediate impulse was to dash into the office to ask for the president. But my training as a hunter had taught me never to rush the victim but to stalk it until it was well exposed and vulnerable.

Guided by these principles, I crossed to the west side of Yonge Street, my heart slowly settling down, to observe the external operations from all angles, while I, myself, remained inconspicuous.

Across the street, I saw the numerous buildings making up the Goodyear complex. So that no one would notice me, I walked slowly by, pretending to window-shop, but all the while I tried to see what was going on inside by looking out of the corner of my eye through the windows of the institution. In this I was unsuccessful. I could not see anything at all. However, I did observe the volume of business carried on externally.

It was impressive and I was proud of Goodyear. They

thought of everything. Who but Goodyear would have thought of including gas pumps for the convenience of their customers, and as part of their operations? And the tires–piles of them– both inside and outside the building! No wonder Goodyear was prosperous! To think that in a short time I would be on their staff.

The thought almost overwhelmed me; at least it took my breath away. Soon I would be a member of the Personnel Relations Department dealing with salaries, negotiating union contracts, talking and laughing with the men.

I walked down to the next intersection, crossed to the east side of Yonge and on the south side of the street running east from Yonge, up Church Street and then westward, until I was again in front of the building of the Goodyear Tire and Rubber Co. There were, as far as I could see, no other entrances to the premises. Nor had I been observed.

Twice more I went around the block, looking at everything before I felt that I was ready to go in.

On the completion of the third circuit, I went boldly to the main entrance and stood near the counter. I was appalled by the general appearance of the vestibule. The floors were greasy; the counter spotted with dark streaks; the chairs were frayed around the edges. Rather than sit, I stood smartly at attention.

I resolved that one of the changes I would recommend to the president in the discharge of my duties was an improvement of the outer offices.

"Whadayawan?" a pimply, sallow-faced youth asked without looking up.

"I wish an audience with your president," I stated with as much authority as I could muster.

The young man paused and choked over the gum which he had been chewing so noisily before I had spoken. He looked at me dumbfounded for a moment, and then, instead of going into the inner sanctum, he went outside, leaving me standing in the vestibule.

Through the plate glass window I could see him whisper to his two companions outside who laughed uproariously as they went about filling gas tanks, opening hoods, extracting caps and then jabbing the innards of the cars with a long metal rod, sometimes nodding, sometimes shaking their heads. The young man I had first spoken to was no longer purple in the face; un-

146

doubtedly he would have to be careful while chewing gum in the future. He looked at me and smirked.

Raging, I stood in the vestibule, plotting ways and means of reporting him to the president on my first opportunity after joining the company. He needed manners.

He came in with a fist full of money, went directly to the cash register, punched it until it rang and the drawer clanked open. As he stuffed in the money, he regarded me quizzically.

"Whatcha say ya wannit?" he inquired.

"I would like an interview with your president." I requested keeping a tight rein on my temper.

Instead of going into the offices he again hurried outside to attend to some business or other. My anger grew.

He returned, followed by two colleagues, one a corpulent youth, the other nondescript.

Going behind the counter, he kicked open the swinging doors and shouted, "Hey, John, there's some guy here who wants to see the president."

The doors closed with a clang. All three grinned at me.

I felt a blush consume my ears; my neck burned.

The swinging doors flew open and a massive man wiping his grimy hands on an equally grimy towel stood enframed. Perspiration dripped down his forehead. His shirt, open at the neck, showed the grizzled hairs on his chest. The sleeves were rolled up over his muscular arms. He glowered at us indiscriminately.

"The president! Sir!" said the young man turning to me with a bow. "This guy wants to see you," he smirked to John.

I was indignant, confused, and crushed. Had the dirty cement floor opened at that moment, I would have gladly sunk in and never asked my destination.

"Yeah?" said he called John. "What can I do for you?"

"I-I-I came to seek–to look for–I want a position–that is a job, with your c-c-company," I stammered.

"Where do you think you are?" boomed Big John over the sniggers of my three tormentors.

"At the Goodyear Tire and Rubber Company, s-s-sir," I managed to stutter.

"Come on, you creeps, get the lead out," Big John commanded his employees, who scurried outside.

Turning to me Big John said, not unkindly, "Son, I'm the owner of this here service station, and you don't look like you want a job here. If you want the Goodyear Tire and Rubber Company, go to New Toronto. I'll tell you how to get there."

"No thanks, Sir," I replied, my knees about to buckle. I backed out of the shop.

"Have a good interview, Sir?" I heard as I retreated.

And I still had to face the Twit before I could get to my room.

PART 4

WITH HOUSING, EDUCATION AND BUSINESS... POOF!

Big Business

Blondie, imported from the State of Georgia by one of our romantic Indians, and inducted into Band membership by way of marriage, was decidedly unhappy with life in general. She had no objection to band membership, but she was no better off as a *bona fide*, registered Status Indian than she had been as a peach-plucking citizen of the United States. Things, in fact, had changed for the worse.

As she contemplated her lot, Blondie fumed. It was cold. The house was small, smaller than the other five houses she and her husband had occupied for varying intervals since they had come to the reserve. The children were sick. They had outgrown their frayed clothing. The food consisted of potatoes, salt pork, gravy and scone, and without any abundance. There were no jobs, only relief and welfare. Worst of all, her husband had been gone all week, and was probably drinking.

The easy life that she had contemplated as the wife of a Status Indian did not exist. Free housing, free medical care, free education, an annuity—hah! Since leaving her beloved Georgia to become a real, registered Indian the only free housing she had seen were the five or six dilapidated old houses that were free to anyone who wanted to occupy them; the only free medical care she and her children had received came from the local, overworked public health nurse who came once a month to dispense pills and demonstrate the proper manner of caring for teeth and hair; free education came from discount, suitcase teachers; and as for the annuity—four dollars—it was "better than other people get." To be the object of envy for exemption from Income Taxation and Realty Assessment would have been nice if income and realty had been forthcoming.

Peach-picking, she decided, was preferable to the precarious and dubious privileges of Indianhood.

When, therefore, Kitche Todosh (Big Tit) came staggering into the house on Sunday night, his bleery-eyes encountered a blustery white woman, Band number 546.

"If you think I'm going to stay on this damned reserve another year, you got another think coming. You'd better get off your butt and find a decent job. We can't live on the fish left in the Bay, or the hunting and fishing, or on cutting pulp wood like you said we could. All we get is relief, relief, and more relief. At least, picking peaches we made some money and fresh fruit."

Kitche Todosh was conciliatory. "Honey, listen to me. What I told you was true. The Bay was once full of trout. The bushes could hardly hide the deer. You could cut pulp and get any job around here. How'se I suppose to know it was gonna change?"

Honey was adamant. "There ain't no fish, no deer, no pulpwood, only relief. I can't stand it any more. You'd better find a job instead of bumming around. If you don't, I'm going back to Georgia."

Kitche Todosh sobered up. He thought about a job. He thought about different jobs. No way was he going back down to Georgia to pick peaches; too damned hot.

Being an enterprising man, Kitche Todosh got a job cutting brush which was sold by the pound to some firm making funeral wreaths. It paid well, but it was damned excruciating work, especially in the winter.

Blondie was satisfied. At least her man was working. Kitche Todosh was less than happy; there were forms of labour more rewarding and less onerous.

Kitche Todosh thought, and eventually he evolved a plan that would bring him financial stability. After he had worked out the details, he outlined his plan to Blondie.

Blondie was aghast. "Bootlegging!" she gasped.

"But it won't be for long, honey, mebee six months, no more," insisted the *entrepreneur*. "And we'll have enough money to buy some equipment, a chain saw, a small truck. Then we'll go into the logging business."

"But suppose you get arrested? You'll have to pay a fine or go to jail or both," Blondie objected.

"Honey, I thought about that; $500 fine or six months or both. Then I got to thinking again. You know these Blunder Bay bootleggers. Well, they get caught once in a while, but they're still in business. Pay the fine and you're back in business the same afternoon. It's sorta like a licence."

"Kinda expensive licence isn't it?" interjected Blondie who could be difficult when investments were to be made without goods actually changing hands. She was far too conservative. And suspicious.

"Listen, honey," said Kitche Todosh getting even more enthusiastic as he warmed to his subject. "It's a risk like everything else. A man going into business has to face risks. Why, he could even get bankrupt. Bootlegging ain't like that, but we still gotta risk something."

Still Blondie hesitated, doubtful. "I don't think it's going to work. Indians around here don't hardly have enough money to eat even. Lots of 'em ain't working either. An' when they do wanna drink they go into town."

Kitche Todosh had done his thinking well; he had researched thoroughly. "Listen, honey." He looked his wife in the eye with appealing honesty while he caressed her skinny hand. "There's more than $70,000 a month in the way of pensions coming into this reserve, and that's not counting baby bonus, mother's allowance or welfare and other stuff. And where does it all go? Blunder Bay. It burns me up to think that we're supporting that town, and all those stores there. Supposing we can get a bootlegging business set up on this reserve, I'm damned sure we can get some of these Indians to spend their money here, and make a good living too."

Blondie argued. She was warming up to the idea, but still hesitated to spend money on less than a sure thing.

"It sounds good, but I'm still afraid. You know people around here. Jealous as hell. If they saw you was doing good, they'd report you to the Provincials."

"Don't worry honey. I thought about that too. We're only gonna have ten or twelve customers that we can trust and who got some money. Can't have everybody, too damned risky. And nobody under age. That's where all the trouble comes in."

Blondie was wavering. "Who are they?" she asked.

"Git a pencil, hon," said Kitche Todosh.

Blondie rummaged in a drawer and came up with a leaky Bic ball point pen.

"Well, there's Mike 'n Norm 'n Bill 'n my brother." He counted them off on his fingers carefully. "Then there's Luffus, 'n Pat. Earl too. 'N Sam, 'n Reg. That otta do it."

"Suppose the police send a spy," worried Blondie.

"And that's the other thing. No white guys. No strangers. That's the policy. Damned good policy. Company policy." Kitche Todosh relished the word "policy." It's officiousness tasted final on his tongue.

"Besides that, we know every guy around here. Recognize any stranger. I ain't scared." said Kitche Todosh defiantly stretching out his legs.

"Where you gonna get the money to start? inquired Blondie coming right to the point.

"I'm getting paid on Friday for that bunch of cedar branches me 'n Norm cut. Getting $50." Kitche Todosh looked pleased.

"But that's our grocery money," wailed Blondie.

"Don't you worry, honey. Figure it this way. I can get ten cases of beer. We can sell it at 70¢ a bottle. That's $16 a case; ten cases at $168; meaning we got a profit of $120."

Blondie opened her eyes wide in surprise at the projected estimate of revenue. It seemed almost too good to be true. She wavered and fell before the logic of good hard cash.

"We still need groceries, hon," she said weakly, by way of capitulation.

"We can get credit at Crooks' in Blunder Bay," Kitche Todosh said knowing her tone for the concession that it was.

"Gee it would be nice to have some money coming in," Blondie whispered going over to her husband and hugging him. Kitche Todosh felt great.

Thursday night Kitche Todosh called on all the friends he placed on his list of preferred patrons. Without reserve every one agreed to come to the launching of his business on Friday night.

On Friday, Kitche Todosh took his $50, hired a cab to take him to town, and returned about an hour and a half later with ten cases of beer.

"Honey," he said to Blondie, "we're going to have a little bit of public relations here. I'm gonna give each one of the guys a free bottle of beer when they come in. That'll get 'em started, 'n after that they gotta pay. You know, honey, I never could figure out why the Commodore and the Algonquin Hotels never gave out a free round. Don't cost them no money, and it's damned good public relations."

Blondie frowned, not quite understanding the finer points of big business, and did some rapid calculations. "Well, O.K.," she agreed at last. Maybe Kitche Todosh was right.

It was shortly after darkness had set in that the patrons arrived.

A car drove up, slowed down; its lights went out. There were voices, cheerful, laughing. A knock.

"Come in."

In they came, five familiar faces, Earl hugging his guitar in his left arm.

"Sid down. Sid down," said their genial host waving an expansive arm. "I'll get you a beer. First round on the house, after that you pay. Seventy cents a bottle. Hey, Blondie, get the boys a drink."

The boys sat down, and Blondie disappeared into the kitchen.

"How much you got, Kitche Todosh?" Norman asked.

"Ten cases!" replied Kitche Todosh proudly.

"Thanks!" said each of the men in turn as he accepted a bottle of free beer from Blondie.

"Should be enough, eh?" Reg commented taking a long and thirsty swig.

"Never get beer at this price in Blunder Bay," volunteered Earl in admiration.

The free round exhausted, the boys began to buy.

"Hey, Kitche Todosh, have one on me!" yelled Reg.

"Me too!" said Pat.

"Me too!" chimed in the others.

Blondie sat five beers at Kitche Todosh's elbow. Business was good. Kitche Todosh had been right; he was a smart man. She grinned at him.

Presently Earl began to play, and then to sing.

Two more cars pulled up and stopped on the road. Five more men appeared, headed by Luffus, completing the list Kitche Todosh had made.

"First round on the house!" shouted Earl before the newcomers had had a chance to sit down.

The new arrivals whistled. "By God, Kitche Todosh, you're a real good guy."

"Come on Blondie, git the boys a free beer. After that it's 70¢ a bottle," Kitche Todosh announced in a friendly, business-like fashion.

Earl resumed his interrupted melody; feet stirred restlessly to accompany the tune. Loud conversation began again.

"Hey! Have a beer on me Blondie," Luffus raised his voice above the din.

"Me too!" came a chorus of ten voices. Blondie set aside the ten bottles. She opened one and took a lengthy pull at the amber foam.

Business was good, better than she had anticipated. She kept busy running back and forth, collecting money and empties, counting out change, putting bills away, opening more bottles, sucking intermittently on her beer.

"Gimme another one," was repeated time and time again. Another bottle, another empty case to be put away. It was good. Money was coming in. There was free beer for her and her husband, which they could turn around and sell a second time. Even entertainment. Pleasing company, and no fights.

"Bring another beer."

Blondie scurried to the kitchen, and back to the living room. Back and forth. Back and Forth. She did not mind it as long as it meant money. Already there was $50 in the drawer, and the prospect of much more to come.

Earl came into the kitchen as she opened yet another bottle.

"Hey, Blondie; I'm broke. Can you give me credit?"

"Dunno. Have to ask Kitche Todosh."

"Hey cus. Com'ere" shouted Earl.

Kitche Todosh got up unsteadily. He had been drinking his free beers. He lurched into the kitchen.

"Hey cuz," said Earl, putting a friendly arm around the neck of his host and kinsman," I'm broke. Can you gimme credit?"

"I guess. Don't like doing it, but I know how it is." Kitche Todosh knew that some businesses depended on credit.

"Blondie, get the scribbler," he said. "Write down Earl's name on a page, and keep a record of all the beers he gets on credit. And Earl, you sign the paper, O.K.? It's a promissory note."

"O.K.," said Earl, taking the pencil and signing his name on the bottom of the hastily made bill.

"Blondie, it's O.K. to give credit to the boys who need it," said Kitche Todosh. "Just make sure you write down all the beers they drink and git them to sign it. Good business practice."

Blondie and Earl looked at Kitche Todosh in awe.

Evidently many of the men had been on the verge of impecuniosity. Dutifully Blondie wrote down their names, each on a separate sheet, recording the number of bottles consumed, and the price of each.

156

The party went on. Kitche Todosh, overwhelmed by the beers that had been purchased for him, fell into a deep stupor and could not be aroused. Blondie and Earl carried him upstairs and stretched him out on the bed.

The party continued as before, Blondie having become the sole host. In deference to her new status, she was presented with a free beer every time she delivered one to a patron. Credit was accumulating; business was thriving. But Blondie was tiring. Moreover she was succumbing to the surfeit of free beer, even as her husband before her.

"Earl! Come here!" she requested finally.

Earl got up and lurched over to Blondie.

"Yeah? What?"

"God, I'm sleepy. I wanna go to bed. Will you look after things down here?"

"Shore!" slurred Earl accommodatingly.

"You know what to do?" inquired Blondie around a yawn she could not stifle.

"Oh, yeah. I do," Earl yawned himself, his eyes watering.

Blondie managed the stairs unaided.

The party went on, a muted roar.

Morning sun awoke Kitche Todosh. He lifted his head from the pillow, and dropped it hastily back, a malicious headache pounding behind his eyes. He reached over and patted Blondie, who, with an equally aggressive hangover moaned, and burrowed her head deeper into the bed clothing.

"How'd we do, honey?" asked Kitche Todosh.

"Fifty dollars cash an' hunnert ten in credit, when I came to bed. Asked Earl to take over. He's your cousin. So sleepy." whispered Blondie before lapsing back into unconsciousness.

"Jeez, that's good. I told you. There's money to be made. Ten more today."

Blondie moaned faintly.

Kitche Todosh was waking up. "I think I'll go down for an eye opener."

So saying he slipped out of bed and went down the stairs.

For a moment all was quiet.

"Hey Blondie!" Kitche Todosh shouted. "There's no more beer, and the list ain't here. Why'd you leave those bastards alone?"

The Kiss and the Moonshine

"Leave women alone and don't drink. Those things can wait. That's how to get an education. That's how the white people do it." Such was the admonition and advice that I received from the elders when I declared my intention to go to school. And so scrupulously did I follow their words that I graduated from Loyola College in Montreal without serious entanglement from either menace.

But it was not always easy to abide by the injunctions of the elders or always to stick to noble resolve especially at a college in Montreal. Abstaining from drink was easy enough; my depleted wallet prevented me from joining the hordes of students who crowded to the bars every Friday afternoon. Women were another matter. And the fact that the faculty members of the college were more than anxious to have their first two pet Ojibway students acquire some social graces and refinement complicated matters that should have been simple.

Induction into white man's ways and customs began almost as soon as my friend and I arrived in Montreal. The first Friday evening we were there, an enterprising faculty member conducted us to the school auditorium where a dance was held for the benefit of in-residence students and the local girls.

We were ushered into the auditorium, introduced to a couple of girls who giggled, and then left to our initiative and devices. My friend, Al, endowed with more initiative than I charged in. I held back to admire the sights. Never had I seen so many young and beautiful women assembled in one place. There must have been two hundred and fifty girls and only about sixty resident freshmen. A man's paradise. Several agonizing foxtrots disclosed to me that most of the women, for that was what I had assumed them to be, were in either grade nine or ten, and by age, just entering puberty.

They had nothing to say to me, nor I to them. They were absolutely disinterested in mining, fishing, timbering and farming. I equally was indifferent to the latest songs, movies, fashions or fads. At age twenty-one, I was too old for them. Deciding to abandon the whole business, I sat down intending to sneak away soon.

My acculturation might have ended then and there had it not been for a very attractive young lady, Jennie by name, who invited me to dance with her.

"Where did you go to school?" she inquired as we floated over the floor.

"In Spanish." I replied.

"Isn't that marvellous! How wonderful!" she cooed.

I was puzzled by her comment, for it had never occured to me that the little Ontario town of Spanish might be extraordinary or exotic.

"What else did you do, while you were at school?" the young thing asked looking into my eyes.

"I worked in the mines and lumber camps," I offered, twirling the young damsel around.

"Oh! you must be strong!" she gushed, looking into my eyes once more, and squeezing my arms. I flexed my muscles, the better to show my prowess.

And so the conversation went–she asking questions–I replying. She listening, while we twirled, skipped, spun and floated around the floor.

"You're a marvellous dancer," she whispered almost breathlessly.

I decided to hang around. There were things I could learn from Miss Charming, even if she were only fifteen and in grade ten. Besides that, she was gracious and gentle.

She took possession of me by seizing my elbow and clinging to me for the balance of the evening. Nor was that the only tangible way she demonstrated proof of her claim upon me. During the course of the evening, my charming companion brought me cakes, cookies, and soft drinks; she even made a lei from the coloured decorative streamers, which she pulled down from the ceiling and wound around my neck. Just the thing that I had been warned against, "watch white women, possessive as anything." I did not mind being possessed, wondering what was so objectionable about it.

Before the dance ended, she asked me to escort her home. I was elated and more than glad to oblige. Out on Sherbrooke Street, we proceeded in an easterly direction toward Girouard. The walk was leisurely and pleasant. But I was startled when my lady-friend quickened her pace, flitted in front of me and veered to my left. But I was just as quick. I too zigged hard left leaving her still to my right side. I was puzzled by this strange manoeuvre, but I promptly dismissed the incident from my mind when she resumed her normal pace and position. She continued to chat, as if nothing had occurred. We had not gone far when my friend darted behind me, emerged on my left and clutched my left elbow from behind before I could recover my senses. I was alarmed and disturbed by this erratic conduct. "What's the m-m-m-matter? I stammered.

"I didn't know how to tell you. I didn't want to hurt your feelings, but in our country, the man always walks on the outside," she purred, squeezing my elbow. I was immediately soothed by her purr.

"Why?" I asked, astounded by a custom about which I had never heard.

"It goes a long way back," she gurgled. "Generations ago, men used to wear swords on the left side. When danger came up, the man simply whipped out his sword with his right hand. If the woman were standing to his right, the man might accidently strike her and put himself at a serious disadvantage."

The explanation was logical but not convincing.

"But men don't wear swords anymore," I muttered.

"Maybe not," Miss Charming countered, "but there was another reason for the custom. A couple of hundred years ago the second floor of houses used to jut out, over and above the street. The occupants of the second floor sometimes threw out their garbage to the street below. Ladies had to walk under the ledge of the second floor to avoid falling refuse."

I was convinced from examination of the architecture of the buildings on Sherbrooke St. that there was no sound reason to perpetuate the custom of a woman walking between escort and buildings. I desisted from telling her about the Indian custom which required women to walk behind men. I let the matter drop and the rest of the walk passed without incident.

At the doorway of her house on Marcil Avenue, she turned and asked me if I would like to come for dinner on Sunday. Gladly and willingly I accepted; and gallantly I shook her hand. While I was shaking her hand she leaned forward and kissed me

160

on the cheek. Overcome, I seized her hand harder and pumped it passionately and romantically. Then I skipped back to the College. This business of getting acculturated was fun.

On Sunday I went to Jennie's house for dinner. She met me at the door, escorted me into the parlour where I met her parents and her sister. A maid in a black uniform and white apron appeared with a tray of glasses.

Jennie's father inquired, "Would you like a drink?"

"Yes, please, I'm thirsty," I replied. The maid brought the tray over. Jennie's father took a small goblet from the tray and handed it to me.

"To your health," he commented, extending his goblet toward me. Not knowing exactly what to do but assuming that he was offering me a second glass as a test of my health and fortitude, I instantly raised my own goblet to my lips, tilted my head back and drained the contents in one draught.

I felt triumphant and I looked to Jennie for some sign of approbation. She only looked aghast. I looked at her father but he had turned his head away slightly and was sipping the wine. Jennie, a glass of orange juice in her right hand, took my elbow with her left.

"Come, I'll show you our library. Father has a large collection of books," she said guiding me around the corner and into a room, where shelf upon shelf sat books on mining and mineralogy.

"He's a mining engineer. I'm sure you'll get along well with him.

"Baz." she said, touching my arm and looking into my eyes, "In our country we sip wine; we don't drink it down like miners or farmers, or Indians." She paused. "You don't mind if I tell you these things. I'm sure you do things differently in your country. But I'll teach you our customs; I'll show you how we do things." She looked at me warmly. I melted.

"No; I don't mind," I assured her. But I was perplexed by her use of the term "our country." Surely I had equal claim.

The maid came in and announced that "dinner is being served." Jennie conducted me to an elegant dining room which was located opposite the parlour. On entry into the dining room we did not sit down immediately but stood behind the chairs. Jennie's father intoned a prayer first. Only when he was seated did the rest of us, as if by signal, sit down.

After I was seated I noticed the disconcerting assembly of brightly polished cutlery surrounding each plate. While I had read of dinners during which one used a startling variety of flatware, I had dismissed such practices as improbable. Now I was confronted by fact. While I was pondering the order of use, the maid returned pushing a cart and set a bowl of clear soup in front of me. Not knowing precisely which spoon to use, I watched Jennie. It was easy; watch and do the same thing. I picked up a round-headed spoon, bent my head over the bowl, and began to scoop out the soup into my mouth.

Jennie placed a hand on my shoulder, whispered softly into my ear, "Watch me." I watched. How graceful and elegant she rendered the act of transferring soup from bowl to mouth. She, like the rest of her family, sat erect, not bent over like me.

In this position, she deftly dipped her spoon into the soup, daintily skimmed the spoon outward and away from the lip of the bowl nearest her, and raised the spoon to her delectable mouth. So simple; and I was a fast learner. I too tried the method. A little awkward perhaps, but I managed. Jennie glanced at me approvingly.

Nor did I realize, until the next course was placed on the table, that meats and roast beef, which were served, were to be eaten with the same flourish and ceremony. Flourish I possessed; ceremony I had not previously observed.

I stabbed a slice of roast beef, cut it violently, shovelled it into mouth and chomped on it vigorously a few times before swallowing it. As I skewered the next portion, Jennie turned to me whispering in my ear,

"In our country, we chew beef fifty-eight times."

Wanting to please her and show that I could adjust to any situation, I promptly began counting with each clamp of my jaws. By this time I had learned to sit upright.

One; two; three; four; five; six; seven . . . .

"Mr. Johnston," Jennie's father intoned, "I understand that you went to school in Spanish. Is that the town near Blind River, Ontario?"

Not knowing which was the greater offence, talking while one's mouth was full or swallowing meat before it was masticated the proper number of times, I was still counting; . . . fourteen, fifteen . . .

"Yes it is, sir." I replied.

"My company, Noranda Mines, is doing some exploratory work in that area. The surveys and core samples are encouraging. You must know the area quite well?"

"Yes, Sir. I worked in lumber camps, just north of Blind

River." I mumbled through a mouth filled with roast beef. I was about to resume chewing the roast beef when I realized to my dismay and in my eagerness to talk that I had forgotten the number of times I had masticated; I could not recall whether it was nineteen or twenty-nine. I wondered what would happen if I underchewed or overchewed the meat. I did not want to start over again; so I started at fifteen.

"Mr. Johnston, I also understand from Jennie that you worked in the mines. Is that correct?" He said.

Twenty-seven, twenty-eight . . .

"Yes sir! I worked for the Algoma Ore Properties, a subsidiary of Algoma Steel." I carefully mouthed my words around the now completely shredded and dry roast beef.

"And what did you do?" He pressed on.

"I worked underground," I rolled the answer over a couple of strands of roast beef.

"Mmmmm, very interesting."

I wanted to eat. I wanted to chew. I wanted to swallow. I forgot how many times I had chewed the beef. With all the questions directed to me, it was impossible to keep count and to think of my answers at the same time. How my hosts managed this, was a wonder to me. White people never ceased to amaze me.

But I gave up; I chewed as discreetly as I could.

"Where were you born?" Jennie's mother asked.

"On the Moose Meat Point Indian Reserve," I replied.

"You're an Indian then!" Jennie's mother said, horror and astonishment in her tone.

"Yes, Ojibway." I answered proudly.

The rest of the meal took on the aspects of an inquisition, but at least some etiquette was forgotten and I was just as glad. I passed the cross-examination with flying colours. So much interest was shown in me that the dinner had become pleasant.

After dinner I lingered another hour answering questions before I excused myself to return to the College and to my studies. I virtually skipped and frisked on the way back like a spring ram.

Next Friday evening I went down to the college auditorium as soon as the doors were opened at 8.00 o'clock. There were crowds of girls, but Jennie was not there; she would, I was certain, arrive later. While I waited, I danced with some of the girls who commented wonderingly upon my Spanish origin. A couple of them even gave me their phone numbers asking me to call them. I accepted the information politely without intending to use it. I much preferred Jennie.

I waited all evening for Jennie who did not arrive. Nor did she ever return to the school dances after that. I wondered why. But all was not exactly lost. During the next few weeks I collected some twenty or twenty-five phone numbers of girls which I dutifully inscribed on the legs of the double decker bed which I occupied.

And just as the faculty members and the local girls were anxious to impart to my friend and me some polish, so were our colleagues. Many of my fellow boarders suggested that I purchase a small black book and write therein the phone numbers and the names of the girls that I had collected. Willing to please and get cultured I bought one, carefully writing down phone numbers only, but not deliberately omitting the names. It was simply a question of economy. I saw no point in depositing all the information especially when I knew which name was associated with which telephone number.

I soon caught on to why my classmates and fellow resident students were so inordinately interested in my book. To confuse them I deliberately set down the names of girls beside the telephone number belonging to other girls. I even added ten or fifteen other fictitious names and numbers to the list. In the end I confounded colleagues and even confused myself.

The girls were possessive as geese, the young men acquisitive as squirrels. But I learned.

I acquired not only some polish and refinement but knowledge over and above the academic. Listening to my colleagues who expounded upon sex once in a while, I came to realize the magnitude of my ignorance in such matters; my inexperience; and the vast knowledge of my colleagues.

Four years at Loyola College went by during which I avoided and evaded women and desisted from alcohol. I became acculturated without catching "culture shock," more or less. I was ready, more or less. I knew something of the theories of romance, and dining and talking more or less.

Even after graduation I was not particularly interested in women nor they in me. Whether they grew weary in the wait or were simply disinterested, I am unable to say; but it was probably for the latter reason.

After I started to work in Toronto, I began going back to the reserve at Moose Meat Point at fairly regular intervals. And I eventually formed a liaison with Early-In-The-Morning, who possessed among other attributes an automobile. She was an Indian girl, in all probability less possessive than her white counterparts; and much less pretentious. Just the girl for me. The elders would approve too. Keep the race pure that way. Each return to the reserve was more pleasant than the last; each held out more promise.

The association with Early-In-The-Morning began innocently enough; but, as I got to know her better, my affection for her grew. So did my resolve to kiss her. However, not knowing precisely how she would respond to my advances, and my amorous fibre being weak and static, Early-In-The-Morning remained unkissed.

I had to do it right. Having learned something about pitching woo and the theory of sex not from gutters or behind barns but from the mouths of the college intellectuals, in sanitary seminar rooms, and in comfortable recreation lounges, I determined that I was well able to apply West European kissing methodology upon Early-In-The-Morning. No more erotic handshakes. But it was rather difficult to decide which approach would best please and most excite Early-In-The-Morning, there being so many ingenious variations to the art of romance. I considered each in turn and dismissed them as somewhat inappropriate. The "Blood-letter," otherwise known as the "hickey rouser" was not the kind of kiss to be rendered at the initiation of a romance. It smacked too much of vampirism and violence. Moreover, Early-In-The-Morning was on the anaemic side. She would not hickey. The "nipper" was too inconstant, missing the point, too birdlike. Besides, Early-In-The-Morning was ticklish; she would probably go into convulsions and terminate the business before it got underway. Then there was "the butterfly" which because I wore glasses would not work. Most intriguing of all was the "French kiss." Were I to try jamming or ramming my tongue into her mouth, Early-In-The-Morning might not be ready for this refined and advanced way of kissing. In all likelihood, she would bite, scream and cause a huge commotion.

While I knew the theory of kissing, I had no real practical experience. Having fastidiously avoided women and girls during my high school and college days, my proficiency in the craft of kissing was deficient. To go out to practise at this point was out of the question.

So I planned a plain simple kiss. Under the circumstances, the gradual approach, as recommended by some of my college contemporaries, was the best. All that remained was the style of kissing. I tried recalling Tom Mix, Hoot Gibson, Roy Rogers and John Wayne, but they were not very illuminating. I went to a few movies and watched Allan Ladd, Glen Ford, Walter Pidgeon and Humphrey Bogart. Of all the kissers I saw, I was most impressed by Humphrey Bogart. His was the technique. It was manly, nothing weak about it; it was honest, nothing deceitful; it was direct, no beating around the bush; and it was forceful, no one could resist it. Early-In-The-Morning would like that. I shivered in excitement. The next time, for sure.

The opportunity came several weeks later, when I again returned to Moose Meat Point ostensibly to visit my parents and relatives. On Saturday I sought out Early-In-The-Morning by walking five miles to her parents' home. She too had come home for the week-end. I was in luck.

That evening we went out to Blunder Bay, and though it was warm I shivered. At the bowling alley, I was unable to hold the ball properly because of the clamminess of my hands. I shivered. Afterwards we went out to a restaurant where I showed her the proper manner of consuming soup, the civilized number of times beef was to be masticated, and the correct posture for dining. For all my guidance Early-In-The-Morning continued to dine without regard for posture or manners or decorum.

"You eat the way you want to eat. I'll eat the way I want to eat," she said. I shivered again. I had but one purpose, one resolve, the kiss. For it, I overlooked her ill-manners and forgave her surliness.

Later that evening Early-In-The Morning took me home, to my uncle's place, where I was staying. All was quiet and in darkness. She stopped at the gate but kept the motor running. We talked. At least she talked; my mouth was too dry for my talking, and I shivered. I moved closer, perhaps a few inches. She talked on, I moved over. She did not seem to notice. Good. She talked on, I moved over again, until I was as close as I could possibly be without sitting on her. Again she did not appear to notice. I took this to mean that she had no objection. So I placed a friendly shivering hand upon her right shoulder. Early-In-The-Morning did not resist. I moved my friendly, shivering, clumsy hand to her other shoulder. She did not protest . . . she did not wince. She was ready. I was ready. She talked on.

I gazed at Early-In-The-Morning. She looked lovely, tempting. She looked at her watch and announced. "My God. I didn't realize it was so late, I'd better get going."

I made my move–manly, direct, forceful and swift– but I did not quite complete the assault for the car horn blasted the stillness of the night and disrupted my ecstasy. I tore myself loose from Early-In-The-Morning, knocking off her hat and getting a button from my coat sleeve entangled in her hair. She screamed. The car horn promptly stopped. The door of the cabin flew open with the reverberating crash of a rifle shot. From the interior, like a bull burst the gangling shape of my uncle, his form made ghostly by his white long johns. On his feet were rubber boots. A cap was jammed over his ears. With a galvanized pail clasped tightly in each hand he scudded across the open field into the mist. Miraculously the light in the cabin was on. I disentangled my button from Early-In-The-Morning's hair. Then she exploded into gales of laughter, rocking and rolling in her seat, while I skulked on my side realizing that I had placed my elbow upon the car horn in my eagerness to kiss her. I slunk out the car door.

I stood unsteadily beside the car, Early-In-The-Morning's peals of laughter stinging my ears. I sort of lurched away. She was still roaring. My ears burned but I no longer shivered. Disconsolately and dejectedly I shuffled toward the cabin.

Early-In-The-Morning tooted her car horn, and then drove off with a roar in a cloud of dust. I was too ashamed to turn around and wave her on her way.

At the door, I waited for my uncle, who emerged from the mists bearing the pails. He was puffing when he came up.

"Oh, its you. Holy Jeez, you scared me. I thought it was the police." Puff, puff, puff. "I just threw out two pails of good moonshine," He said mournfully, puffing and wheezing some more. I dared not disclose my own misadventure.

"We would'a had a nice drink," he grumbled.

"Yeah; too bad," I commiserated.

As it was there was no kiss and no moonshine.

A Sign of the Times

A special meeting to which Ojibway and Cree chiefs from all over Northern Ontario were invited was convened by the Department of Indian Affairs. The meeting was to be held in the basement of the local Baptist church, the Catholic church basement being too small to accommodate the expected number of guests and the entire population of Moose Meaters who were sure to turn out.

No one knew what was to be discussed, but everyone was certain that whatever it was must be of high importance because the Regional Director of Indian Affairs himself was going to be present, an unheard of event. Besides this eminent personage there were to be representatives from the Indian Affairs Branch in Ottawa, delegates from the Ontario Departments of Lands and Forests, Health and Social Services, and Education. To be added to this imposing array were emissaries from the Union of Ontario Indians, the National Indian Brotherhood, the Indian-Eskimo Association and the Society of Friends. Swelling this group were anthropologists, ethnologists, sociologists and linguists from different universities and museums across Ontario. A battery of interpreters rounded out the official party. Everyone in Moose Meat Point guessed at the purpose of the gathering; some were very suspicious; everybody grew excited as they awaited the greatest of days.

On the morning of the appointed day, Moose Meaters congregated in little crowds along the dusty road that led down to the wharf in a little bay. They did not have long to wait. Around 10.00 o'clock, Beaver and Otter aircraft, generously provided by the Ontario Department of Lands and Forests, landed in the bay, taxied to the wharf where they disgorged their cargo of some fifty officials.

The chief and his Band Council greeted the entourage with handshakes, smiles and with a few grunts thrown in, before conducting them toward the Baptist church.

In the church basement the chief and Councillors ushered the suited visitors to a great long table that had been installed at one end of the basement hall. Only about thirty of the fifty guests from the outside world could be seated at the table of honour; the others had to sit on benches immediately in front of the conference table. The five interpreters were installed in a special table located to the left of the conference table. Those of the Moose Meaters who could get into the hall sat on benches behind the guests and against the walls; the rest had to stand at the doorway and outside. A few resourceful ones opened transoms from the outside and lying on their stomachs peered in.

As soon as everyone was seated, the chief, as the official host, welcomed the guests on behalf of the Moose Meat Point Indian Reserve. Then he turned the chair over to Alben Iron Lung one of the smart Indians from Southern Ontario.

"Ladies and Gentlemen," Alben Iron Lung began in English because he could talk neither Cree nor Ojibway. "On behalf of my colleagues and friends I would like to express the depth of the emotion we all felt by the genuine warmth of your reception and the charm of your village. You may justly be proud of your achievements and your community. It is because you value your heritage and recognize the merits of change that we come to you."

"Today the native people begin a new era," he continued. "Today marks the inception of a new and exciting relationship and partnership between the Indian Affairs Branch and the native peoples of this province and this country. For from this day forward there is to be consultation between the federal government and the native peoples. No more will decisions be made arbitrarily or unilaterally."

"Jist a minute, here!" one of the interpreters broke in, holding up his arm to halt the chairman. The chairman broke off his stream of oratory.

"You're goin' too fas," the interpreter complained. "We gotta translate 'new an' excitin' relationship and partnership, an arbitr .. an! what was dat udder big word you used?"

"Unilaterally," the chairman repeated.

"Yeah! dat's it. What's dat mean?" the interpreter inquired.

"It means," the chairman explained, "one side only; in this particular instance, a decision made without consultation, by one party only."

"Oh!" was all the interpreter could manage. And he bent his head forward, slouched his shoulders in huddle with his colleagues. After several minutes of head wagging and nodding, interspersed with grunts of "Kaw (no)," two interpreters, one Cree and one Ojibway, got up and made fiery speeches of differing durations. The members of the audience looked at one another and nodded, while the visiting delegates applauded as if they understood.

"Okay! You can keep on, but don' go too fas'," the Cree interpreter pleaded.

The chairman smiled and resumed as if he had not been interrupted. "This day may also inaugurate the commencement of a new program for the native people of this nation who have long been neglected. Before I ask the Regional Director of Indian Affairs to explain the program I would like to introduce the distinguished members that make up the official party. I would ask you to refrain from applauding until all the guests have been introduced." The interpreters translated. No one applauded as the chairman named the participants along with their functions. At the end of the litany, there was a tremendous burst of applause.

"I now present to you Mr. Oscar Blusker, the Ontario Regional Director for the Indian Affairs Branch," and the chairman sat down smugly.

"Mr. chairman," Mr. Oscar Blusker clipped his words and stretched a smile, "my friends. For some years now, the government and my Department have been aware of the dreadful living conditions prevailing in many Indian communities. Housing is sub-standard; existing homes, research has shown, consist in 90 per cent of the cases of only one room with no private quarters. And most lodgings are constructed of either tar paper or logs. Moreover, on this reserve as with most Indian communities, the houses have no indoor sanitary or plumbing facilities; few have electricity; none enjoy telephone communications. Research conducted by sociologists indicate that there is a direct relationship between housing, employment, academic achievement, and numerous social problems. The average annual individual income is the lowest in the country, and in many cases, welfare constitutes the only source of income. Alcoholism is emasculating our native people and there are more native people *per capita* involved in conflicts with the law than any other group."

The Regional Director was interrupted by the chief interpreter who shot his hand up over his head, "Hold it! Jist a minute." All the interpreters bent their heads forward, whispering furiously or grunting in neutral tones. From time to time there could be heard, "No! He didn't say dat," "Buzz . . . " "No! He didn't mean dat. Buzzzzzzz . . . You can't say it like dat. Buzzzz." A hand shot up. "Hey! What does emusculate mean? How'd you say it?"

The Regional Director looked at the chairman. The chairman rose from his seat, smiling and in a very grave manner gave a learned explanation, "It means to weaken by cutting off the testicles."

The interpreter looked shocked, "Is that what happens when people drink?" he inquired.

"Of course," the chairman said with certainty and finality.

The interpreter turned to his colleagues said something in Ojibway. An Ojibway turned to his Cree partner who looked startled and frightened. Together they consulted and then smirked, then giggled, and then "haw, haw, haw," they all roared. The Regional Director looked chagrined. The Moose Meaters looked puzzled; the linguists wrote furiously. One of the interpreters stood up and addressed the chair. "I don' tink, we can say dat, us. Mean sometin' else."

The chairman grinned, "In the context in which the Regional Director was speaking," he said, "the term means weakening of the will, resolve and pride and determination of those who drink to excess."

"Oh!" the interpreter grunted seeming to be satisfied. The interpreters huddled once more, shaking and wagging their heads. At the end of ten minutes of gesticulating and mumbling, the two chief interpreters stood up and both delivered short impassioned speeches. The audience, looking bewildered, nodded. The interpreters signalled the Regional Director to continue.

Mr. Blusker outlined the new programs which the Indian Affairs Branch had evolved for the solution of all Indian housing problems. He explained that there were four distinct aspects to the overall plan. The first would be known as on-reserve housing. By this plan, houses complete with electrical and plumbing facilities and divided into rooms much like urban dwellings would be constructed on the reserve for those who qualified. Funding for the housing program would be provided by the Branch and repaid by the Indians over a specified period until the mortgage was paid off. The scheme, he went on, would operate very much like other standard mortgage practices. Mr. Blusker paused to allow the interpreters to convey the substance of his remarks. While the interpreters gabbled among themselves, the Director lit his pipe and the linguists wrote furiously. It was a while before the interpreters agreed upon a suitable translation.

Continuing, Mr. Blusker outlined the mechanics of off-reserve housing. He said that the Department would finance for Indian peoples, who qualified, the purchase of dwellings in nonreserve areas such as large cities. Any native person residing and gainfully employed in a metropolitan area would be eligible for a mortgage loan that would be repaid at a rate of interest lower than conventional rates. Mr. Blusker again paused to allow the interpreters to digest and rephrase his remarks in Cree and in Ojibway. He smiled.

One of the interpreters gasped, "Holy Smokes" expressing the astonishment of his colleagues. There was another animated discussion before the interpreters explained the gist of Mr. Blusker's revelations. The audience appeared neither pleased nor displeased; the Ojibway and Cree remained stoical, just like Indians. They continued to puff on their pipes and cigarettes filling the hall with a fog of blue smog.

The Regional Director resumed. He declared that there was one other dimension to the overall plan. According to the village relocation plan, an entire community could be relocated in a different site within a reserve, new homes constructed and the old demolished.

Mr. Blusker went on to say that he believed that on-reserve housing and village relocation plans would be of special interest and application to Moose Meat Point because studies and research conducted by the provincial and federal governments indicated that the present village site was no longer viable. Over the years, the water wells had dried up and the soil had become exhausted. He pointed out that the same studies had shown that there was on the reserve a more favourable site ten or twelve miles farther to the west.

The Regional Director smiled elastically as he warmed up to the advantages to be gained by relocation. He promised that a new road would be built enabling buses to transport the village children to schools in Blunder Bay. Construction of homes would provide employment and income. New dwellings with all the amenities would enhance the academic performance of students. He said that with adequate housing, sociologists had found that all the problems would vanish "poof." So many advantages and benefits to be gained. The Indian Affairs Branch had not been remiss in the discharge of its responsibilities as critics had been wont to say.

Mr. Blusker assured the audience that the decision to relocate was entirely up to the Band Council. His department would in no way interfere. But should the Moose Meat Point Indians decide upon relocation, Indian Affairs would assist in every manner possible, providing money, technical advice and expertise for the entire project. The Regional Director's mouth stretched rubber band-like into a benign smile. "I thank you for your patience in listening to such a dry explanation," he said as he sat down.

For what seemed like minutes the interpreters gaped open-mouthed at the Regional Director. Then as one, they collectively hunched their shoulders, drew their heads in like turtles and began a fierce debate which was punctuated with the shaking of heads, and the wagging of fingers while the visitors fidgeted, the linguists scribbled, and the Moose Meaters smoked. For a few moments it appeared that the interpreters would fight among themselves. Eventually they settled whatever differences they may have had and appeared to agree. The two senior interpreters lurched to their feet and addressed the enthralled audience.

The visitors applauded; the Moose Meaters continued to smoke. In the silence the chairman interposed with, "Are there any questions?" And he looked around to see if there were any Indians who might be unclear as to what had been said. But the Moose Meaters puffed placidly on. Mr. Iron Lung tried again, "If there is something you do not understand, please feel free to ask for clarification. Now is the time, not later. Now is the time to ask questions of our delegates, experts and resource persons. Tomorrow will be too late, they will be gone." The linguists scribbled. The Moose Meaters appeared content.

One Cree delegate from James Bay raised his hand which the chairman readily recognized by saying, "There is a question from the floor. Sir would you please give your name, occupation, capacity and state your question." A Cree interpreter interpreted; the linguists scribbled.

The Cree who had raised his hand spoke in his language

173

giving a ten-minute impassioned speech. Everyone was spellbound. When he finished, the visitors, none of whom understood a word, applauded mightily. The linguists scribbled vigorously.

A Cree interpreter got up. "His name is Samson Achooshoo; she's trapper, she's wann'a know what dem udder guys are doin' here." The interpreter sat down.

The chairman asked each visitor to stand and to introduce himself or herself and to state their functions, and for the interpreter to translate simultaneously. For the most part the self-introductions were received without comment and proceeded smoothly and quickly enough.

"My name is Ernest Menominee. I'm the president of the Union of Ontario Indians. Our organization will assist you in resolving any disputes you may have with Indian Affairs." The big man sat down to warm applause.

Without waiting for the chairman a hefty lady rose to her feet. "I'm Big Flossie. I'm Councillor here on dis reserve. I wanna know how can youse guys find time to help us fight Indian Affairs when youse guys is fightin' amongst yourselves?" She sat down and adjusted her faded tam. Ernest Menominee grimaced; a Cree interpreter muttered a few words.

After a few more guests described themselves, an elderly matron, hair streaked with blonde got up at the official table. "My name is Olga Shaposhnikoff employed by the Ontario Department of Health. The Department will assist in family planning and provide diet and nutrition courses." She slithered back into her seat, and smiled. Her message was translated into Cree and Ojibway. The linguists scribbled some more.

Big Flossie got up again. "I wanna ast dat woman some questions," she said tugging at her tam.

"By all means," the chairman acknowledged, "that's what she's here for."

"Mrs., whatever you name is," she did not quite finish. . . .

"It's Miss Olga Shaposhnikoff," the lady from the Health Department broke in somewhat coldly.

"How many kids you got?" Big Flossie demanded.

"Why? What has that got to do with the services our Department can offer and render?" Miss Shaposhnikoff stammered.

"Look Miss whatever you name is," Big Flossie shot in, placing her hands on her hips and scowling at the same time. "Don' git smard wid me; maybe old me, but I kin skin you any-day. Jis remember dat. Always de same. White peoples come 'ere tells us poor Indians what to do, ast us questions. An' when us Indians ast questions, youse neber answer. Dis time youse gonna answer. De chairman up dere said youse peoples gonna answer."

"Maybe Miss whatever you name is, you kin get away wid dat wid de mens aroun' here. Dey is scared; just sit dere an lissen an' say nudding. Well, dey kin jis sits dere like sheeps. Not me. I'm not scaret of dem, me. I'm not scaret of you neider. So Miss whatever you name is jis' remember dat dis is my reserve an' if you don' answer my questions, I fin' you outside apter, and I'll shake some answers from you. Now. How many kids you got?"

"None," Miss Shaposhnikoff spluttered.

"Dats bedder! You married, you?" Big Flossie examined.

"No," Miss Shaposhnikoff answered in a quivering voice.

"You take dem pills, you?" Flossie interrogated.

"No," Miss Shaposhnikoff replied, quaking.

"Den, how come youse gonna teach us dis family planning. Youse aint married; youse ain't got kids; youse don' take pills; youse don' hab a house. How you gonna teach us dem tings? Eh? Eh? Eh?"

"I read and do research," Miss Shaposhnikoff returned.

"Well, me, I don't hab no education. I raisit ten kids. I keep house, I keep clean. I feed my husband. I happy me. You happier, you, wid no kids? Is womens who hab no kids happier? Only time us take pills and medicine is w'en wese sick. Is dat de bes' your department can do? If dat's de bes', den we don' need you dammed help." Big Flossie sat down. The interpreters went to work. Miss Shaposhnikoff blanched and paled. The Indians applauded. Several more guests introduced themselves and explained their works.

"I'm Dr. Eunice Fanny from the University of Toronto, where I teach Cree. Previously to my current appointment I taught Ojibway at the University of Calgary. I'm here to learn the various Cree and Ojibway dialects, and help in the development of language courses and curricula," the scrawny lady lisped.

Big Flossie was up on her feet again. "Mr. chairman," she said addressing the chair, "I'd like to ast dat woman a coupla questions. Whats dat ling . . . How'd you says it?" She appealed.

"Linguistics. It means the study of languages. And this lady specializes in Ojibway and Cree," the chairman clarified.

"Oh good!" purred Flossie "Neber saw white mans who speak Indian, me. Very glad to see one who speak my language. Eberybody who come 'ere speak English. I speak my own language now." and Big Flossie poured into Ojibway. The interpreters sat back. Big Flossie ranted on for fifteen minutes or so; she ended by saying "Now whad you say to dat?"

Dr. Fanny rose unsteadily to her feet. "I don't understand your dialect, it's more Cree than Ojibway."

Big Flossie growled, "Whaddaya mean you don' unnerstood! and I don' like you making fun of my language. I don' mix up no Cree wid my Ojibway. I thought you was smart teaching Cree and Ojibway. You can' unnerstand no Cree and no Ojibway." Big Flossie got angrier and angrier. She raised her voice. "Which dialec' you wan'. We got lots of Crees and Ojibways here. Which one do you wan', pick anyone. Which one? eh? Which one?" and Big Flossie put her hands on her hips again and glowered at Dr. Fanny who shuddered.

"I'm afraid I don't speak either language," she admitted reddening.

Flossie harrumphed, "I don' know why youse here. Preten' you knows our language; can' even unnerstand a word. You can' help us no ways. Don' know why youse is here. Always preten's youse knows more dan us. Don' need none ob youse here."

"Madame Councillor," the chairman interjected coming to Dr. Fanny's rescue, "There is much business to attend to; many more people to introduce before we come to the real purpose of the meeting. But I am glad that you speak frankly and express your sentiments in such a forthright manner. It is good that you do so but we must move on."

Several more people, with less assurance or aplomb than their other colleagues had previously shown, introduced themselves, stating their business, conscious of Big Flossie's presence. Flossie, arms folded, simply lurked on the bench.

"I'm Dr. Wilbur Livingston-Bull, biologist with the Division of Wildlife Services, Ottawa. My associates and I would like to study the changes in the habits and movements of the deer population of this area that may be brought on by the relocation of your community. Should you agree to relocation and should you consent to a study of the kind we envisage and propose, my department would send in scatological researchers to begin work this summer. During the course of our field work we would of course consult and co-operate with you. At the end of our research, which we intend to conclude in about two years, we would donate several copies of our published reports to your library."

The guests applauded the generosity of the scientist from the Division of Wildlife Services. Such an offer had never before been made. Dr. Wilbur Livingston-Bull smiled. The Moose Meaters kept puffing placidly.

An interpreter stabbed the air with a hand.

"Yes," the Chairman said.

"We wanna know what dat word means, seat . . . scat . . . before we can interpret," the interpreter appealed.

"Scatology is the science or the study of either human or animal waste; faeces; droppings," the chairman explained. "Scatologists can tell from deer droppings changes in the eating habits and in the basic diet of deer; they can also determine the movement of deer from scatological evidence."

The interpreters' eyebrows lifted and arched in astonishment and shock. Those eyebrows sagged and spread while mouths extended into grins. The interpreters snorted, sniggered and chortled. Both Cree and Ojibway interpreters stifled chuckles as they explained about the deer.

Moose Meaters, men and women, were aghast at this novel form of study. One was heard to exclaim "Sahh! Weenziwuk (How dirty)." The comment was greeted by laughter. Big Flossie looking thoroughly disgusted boomed out, "Sounds like a lot of sh–– to me!" and she stomped out as the audience roared. Dr. Wilbur Livingston-Bull reddened.

Soon after that the introductions ended and the meeting recessed for lunch. After lunch the meeting resumed without Big Flossie and without interruption. At the end of the deliberations the Moose Meat Point chief delivered a speech, part in English, part in Ojibway, that his council would certainly consider the Indian Affairs Branch proposals. He ended by saying, "If you're satisfaction, I'm satisfaction too." Everyone cheered and applauded the sentiment.

That night there was a huge banquet, with moose meat and wild rice for the visitors. Early next morning Beavers and Otters flew in, ingested the visitors and took them away to the south.

Within a week following the departure of the visitors, the Moose Meat Point Band Council met to consider the proposals of the federal government. Everyone in the community was invited to attend and to speak out. Catholics, Baptists, a few pagans, Liberals, Conservatives, New Democrats, Socialists, Capitalists, progressives and traditionalists turned out for the meeting.

Old wounds were re-opened; some new ones were inflicted; none were healed. The Baptists, relying on irrefutable biblical evidence, argued that it was immoral for people to abandon their homes in order to acquire new ones; progressives, mainly the young, countered by saying that "you can't live in the past, you gotta progress in order to move ahead." Big Flossie, a sort of traditionalist retorted on behalf of the older people, "Youse young peoples, alls you tink about is progress. You tink we neber heard of dat, us, eh? Well, Indians tought about progress long times ago; before youse was borned. Married the whites, dem; moved off de reserve, dem. Got Métis kids. Didn' do dem any good. Jis ast de Métis. Don' eben talk Indians youse. Dat progress eh? eh? Eh? Do you any good jus' to speak English eh? eh? Like you any bedder, dem? eh? eh? Alls we do now is talk, talk, talk, in Council. Alls I wan' is a house and talk neber got me anyting. It's work, work, work. Alls we gotta do today is decide youse wanna house or youse don' wanna house. Yes or No. We di'nt come 'ere for make big speeches." Turning to the chief, Flossie suggested, "Chief! sooner we vote, sooner we gits houses, us. We's waste lotsa time talking; deres lotsa work at home."

The chief, saying that Councillor Flossie made a lot of sense, called for a vote by secret ballot. Pieces of paper were distributed to all present who were instructed to write "yes" or "no" on the slips. When this was done, the ballots were counted and the secretary announced the results; 40 per cent for, 38 per cent against, with 22 per cent abstentions.

The chief was pleased. He declared with pride that Moose Meat Point was not as unprogressive as some might have suggested that morning during the discussions. That the Council operated on democratic principles and had elected to investigate modern housing and facilities were evidence of the progressive spirit of the Moose Meat people. The chief assured the crowd that negotiations with the Indian Affairs Branch would begin immediately. The meeting adjourned.

As promised, discussions with the Indian Affairs Branch began almost at once. The reluctant Ojibway of the Moose Meat Point Reservation were persuaded by the promise of new houses, similar in style, appearance, and appointment to those occupied by white people in non-Indian communities, to abandon their one-room log and tar paper shacks. In addition to three and four bedroom dwellings with hydro, and plumbing, roads were to be constructed.

Consent obtained, Indian Affairs Branch was hugely pleased. It would show those urban, know-nothing critics that the Department was not remiss or inactive, but that it was doing something for its charges, albeit quietly.

Almost immediately after consent to move was obtained, a few Indians who were deemed to be bright were given a crash course in all aspects of carpentry—the proper procedure in pummelling nails, the correct manner of holding the hammer, saw, and screwdriver. Nothing was left to chance. A couple of the smarter Indians were flown off the reserve and taken to a small town Community College to learn advanced carpentry, masonry, and blueprint reading. In the meantime, the Indian Affairs Branch Town Planners sketched plans, conferred with the Moose Meat Point Band Council for approval, and eventually came up with a town plan which obtained approving nods from the chief and Council. An entire summer and winter had gone by.

By spring, everything was ready. The plans were delivered in handsome round rolls, white lettering set on a blue background. The two clever Indians returned, and were promptly appointed Head Carpenter and Assistant Head Carpenter by Band Council resolution. An Indian Affairs Branch engineer arrived to supervise all operations and construction. Within a few days, small Otters and Beavers flew in with enough material for the building of forty units, and flew back out for more.

The Chief Engineer, Mr. Shastu Karoom Varoon was immensely pleased by the smoothness of the operation. He turned to the chief standing beside him as they watched the intense energy with which the Indian workmen set about the task of clearing the land.

"Its a great day, a good beginning, a new era," he extolled expansively, unable to express his elation in a single word.

Around him men slashed and bashed with axes and saws to clear the land.

"Yeah!" agreed the chief, spitting.

Karoom Varoon could hardly contain himself. Thrusting his fingers into his waistcoat pockets and assuming a stance he had always considered suitable for a man of great affairs, he said, "Chief, only through co-operation and consultation between your people and the Department is a project such as this possible." His eyes flashed, and his teeth sparkled in a vast smile. He clapped the chief's shoulder. "Isn't that right, chief?"

"What?" the chief asked, neither understanding the lilting accent of Pakistani, nor the terms Karoom Varoon used.

"Working together!" the engineer explained, more loudly in an attempt to overcome the language barrier. This the chief understood.

"Yeah!" he agreed.

"And we didn't receive any help from our critics, either," Karoom Varoon added.

"Who?" the chief asked getting angry. "Who send crickets? Don't need any more crickets, us. Eat everything. Damn bugs."

"People who complain," said Karoom Varoon by way of explanation.

"Yeah!" the chief grunted, with a nod. Who was complaining?

The land was cleared. The foundations were dug. Cement was poured. All summer the northern tamarack forest reverberated with the bang and clang of hammers, and the buzz of saws.

At summer's end, the houses were complete and ready for occupancy. The Ojibway moved in. The engineer left for Toronto, his work complete. Not long afterward, the two principal carpenters left to seek employment elsewhere.

Of course, the Moose Meat Point Band was happy with the brand new bungalows even though none had the inside facilities which had been promised. Who were they to complain? Would it not be the height of ingratitude to plead for and bemoan the lack of bathrooms when houses were supplied? They were more than grateful . . . and enterprising.

As they had done in the past, the Moose Meat Point Ojibway constructed their own outdoor conveniences by attaching a cross-piece nailed at a suitable height to two trees growing three or four feet apart, and digging a pit some six feet in depth below the bar. Over this they placed a rude roof. No problem.

Life went on blissfully to that winter. But in the latter part of January, several Beaver and Otter flew back in and landed on the ice with loads of more building materials, which several perplexed Ojibway unloaded and placed on the ice. The pilots promptly betook themselves to the air, heading in the general direction of the south, leaving no word except that the material was from Indian Affairs. No one, not even the chief, knew what the lumber was for.

Consequently the material sat on the ice in neat little piles for several days. The Band Council met to discuss the matter, but remained undecided as to the disposition of the timber.

Some of the Council members argued unsuccessfully that to do nothing would be a reflection on their initiative. Others argued that it would be wiser to await instructions. This opinion prevailed. As a result the Council, by overwhelming majority passed a resolution to await for further instructions.

However, one bold and enterprising Indian managed to figure out how to put the materials together. Without authority, he made a little hut. Following his example, the other villagers put together more timbers and boards and constructed similar small houses on the lake. Soon forty small edifices stood on the ice near the shore. The chief and Council were powerless to prevent initiative and industry.

Spam Scurry, an official with the Department of Lands and Forests, surveying the area in a Norseman on behalf of the Ontario Provincial government was appalled at the sight below him. Forty toilets on Porcupine Yellow Liver Lake. Indians scudding back and forth from the village to the huts, from the huts to the village.

Directing the pilot to return to base immediately, Spam wired the government offices in the district to relay the message to Sault Ste. Marie, which in turn conveyed the intelligence to Toronto. The Assistant Deputy Minister eventually found the Deputy Minister in a meeting in Napanee. The Deputy Minister wired the Minister who was holidaying in Hawaii. The Minister telegraphed back:

INFORM INDIAN AFFAIRS BRANCH stop REQUEST THAT INDIANS CEASE CONTAMINATING LAKE stop

A week later the Deputy Minister found time to draft an urgent memorandum to the Regional Director, Indian Affairs Branch in Toronto.

Dear Sir:

Please be advised that the Native people of the Moose Meat Point Indian Reserve have improperly and without authority erected forty privy structures upon the ice surface of Porcupine Yellow Liver Lake contrary to regulations. The frequency of usage, as reported by one of our senior officials, indicates that the lake is contaminated and that the residents of the community are in all likelihood infected with an intestinal disease. It is imperative for the continued quality of the lake and the good health of the residents, that the Indians remove the offending privies and use the indoor conveniences that have been provided for them. Immediate action to this request is earnestly solicited,

Sincerely,
S.M.A. Barnmutter.

The Regional Director was horrified. He hastily convened a staff meeting asking for guidance. He then fired off a terse memorandum to the Assistant Deputy Minister. The Assistant Deputy Minister located the Deputy Minister, after a frantic search, attending a meeting in Yellowknife. On his own initiative the Assistant Deputy Minister managed to get a message through to the Minister who was attending a Lion's Club conference in Charlottetown. A response came back.

Get the Indians and their privies off the lake immediately.

R.A. Canse.

On receipt of the authority to act, the Ontario Regional Director of Indian Affairs, along with Spam Scurry, an engineer, and an official from the Department of Health chartered a Norseman to fly them to Porcupine Yellow Liver Lake.

As they descended, they observed the forty huts on the lake, with many of the residents entering and going out of the edifices. They were convinced. The lake was contaminated and the Indians were afflicted.

They landed. The Regional Director wasted no time in getting out of the plane and racing to the nearest hut. He was furious, yet at the same time he was sorry for the poor Indians in their trouble. Moreover he was polite. His genteel habits did not allow him to walk into a toilet unannounced. Therefore, when he came to the privy door, he knocked.

"Peendigaen (Come in)," came a cheerful voice.

The Regional Director cautiously opened the door and looked into the smiling face of an Indian who was kneeling in front of the bench jiggling a fishing line through the hole in the toilet seat. In one corner of the hut was a pile of whitefish. The Regional Director's mouth gaped open. He was unable to speak.

"You from Gummint, I guess, eh?" said the Indian.

"Boy, Gummint real good. Real nice house for ice fishing.

Only one thing. Holes are too small for some big fish. You t'ink dey can fix dat, eh?"

He continued to jiggle his line with his right hand as he went about the business of fishing.

EPILOGUE

EPILOGUE

All the stories recounted in this book are true: all are based on events that have occurred. (The names of the principals in the stories have been changed.) If the accounts sometimes appear to be far-fetched and even implausible, it is simply because human beings very often act and conduct their affairs and those of others in an absurd manner.

Some of the events recorded are the products of Ojibway impulsiveness; others are the result of misunderstanding, or imperfect communication of information; still others are the consequence of the application and clash of different cultural approaches.

Ojibway and other native North Americans will readily recognize and appreciate the stories for what they represent. In order for those with different cultural backgrounds to grasp the substance of the stories, they must understand the influence and role of missionaries and bibles upon Ojibway belief; comprehend the power and force of the Indian Agent and the Indian Act upon the life of the Ojibway; know the attitudes and the character of the English-speaking West European and his regard for other peoples; and finally be aware of the ever-shifting trends in policies and practices of governments in their dealings with the native peoples.

A case in point is contained in "A Sign of The Times." Prior to the 1960s, all decisions respecting policy and program were made by the Indian Affairs Branch and presented as *fait accomplis* to the native peoples. Commencing around the 1960s, a new approach, reflecting an enlightened attitude and a more generous spirit was injected into government-Indian relationships. Indians were consulted on many matters concerning their well-being before decisions were rendered. Whenever a new program was to be instituted or some important issue to be resolved, general meetings were convened, to which all sorts of officials, chiefs, delegates, and interpreters were invited, equipped with cameras and tape recording machines. There was no real pattern to the meetings; the course of many meetings followed the order described.

The few accounts recorded in this book have for years amused the Ojibway of Moose Meat Point. The events and their repeated telling can reflect and reveal only one aspect and only a small portion of the Ojibway sense of humour. The stories as written cannot adequately convey the real nature or impart the scope of that sense of wit and humour that forms an integral part of the Ojibway peoples and their character. The limits of translation act as an effective bar to a fuller exposition of Ojibway humour.